Warman's
LALIQUE

Identification and Price Guide

©2004 Krause Publications

Published by

 **krause publications**
An imprint of F+W Publications, Inc.

700 East State Street • Iola, WI 54990-0001
715-445-2214 • 888-457-2873
www.krause.com

Our toll-free number to place an order or obtain
a free catalog is (800) 258-0929.

Library of Congress Catalog Number: 2004103297

ISBN: 0-87349-787-2

Designed by Kara Grundman
Edited by Dennis Thornton

Printed in the United States of America

Warman's Lalique Identification and Price Guide

Table of Contents

The Lalique Mystique

To say that René Lalique was a gifted artist is something of an understatement. Lalique was that rare combination of design genius and prolific innovator, whose creations brought him acclaim during his lifetime, and whose legacy is still the focus of collector fascination today.

Think of this: At age 47, when many men would be looking down the road to retirement after decades of creative endeavors, he launched a glass-making empire that is without equal. And then, less than a score of years after his death, he was almost forgotten.

Despite the attacks of critics like architect Adolf Loos, who in 1908 decried the influence of the art nouveau movement in general, the environment in which Lalique thrived was one that nurtured some of the greatest design trends in the new 20th century. Lalique was in distinguished company.

When he opened his glass factory in 1907, Lalique's contemporaries included another influential glassmaker, Emile Galle; American designer Louis Comfort Tiffany; Antoni Gaudi, the great Spanish architect; Alphonse Mucha, the Czech printmaker; Gustav Klimt, the Austrian painter, and Charles Rennie Mackintosh, the Scottish designer.

Like the cryptic images of M.C. Escher, which morph from simple drawings to living creatures to fantasy and back, Lalique's menagerie was a constantly evolving brood of vegetation, insects, fish, birds, and beasts, overseen by a chorus of romantic figures. It seemed there was no facet of the natural world that Lalique couldn't transform into objects of color and light that are anything but utilitarian:

The swarming school of fish that encircles "Formose."

The regal grasshoppers captured on "Sauterelles."

The mute parakeets sitting like sentinels on "Ceylan" and "Perruches."

It's amazing to think of it now, but by the mid-1950s, the works of Lalique and his contemporaries were widely regarded as no more than a footnote in design history. The creations that had seemed so revolutionary and stunning in the first quarter of the 20th century were now seen as quaint and outdated reminders of an era between the World Wars.

It was not until the late 1960s and early '70s that a devoted group of collectors emerged to put Lalique's work into the proper perspective. This book is dedicated to their scholarship.

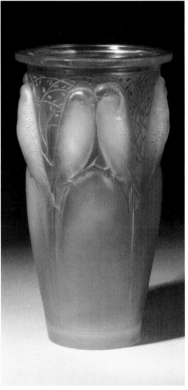

"Ceylan"

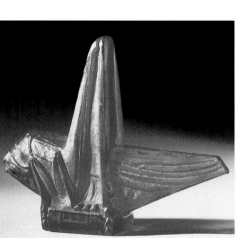

"Formose"

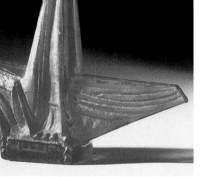

"Sauterelles."

"Perruches"

René Lalique, 1860-1945

René Jules Lalique was born on April 6,1860, in the village of Ay, in the Champagne region of France. In 1862, his family moved to the suburbs of Paris.

In 1872, Lalique began attending College Turgot where he began studying drawing with Justin-Marie Lequien. After the death of his father in 1876, Lalique began working as an apprentice to Louis Aucoc, who was a prominent jeweler and goldsmith in Paris.

Lalique moved to London in 1878 to continue his studies. He spent two years attending Sydenham College, developing his graphic design skills.

He returned to Paris in 1880 and worked as an illustrator of jewelry, creating designs for Cartier, among others. In 1884, Lalique's drawings were displayed at the National Exhibition of Industrial Arts, organized at the Louvre.

At the end of 1885, Lalique took over Jules Destapes' jewelry workshop. Lalique's design began to incorporate translucent enamels, semiprecious stones, ivory, and hard stones.

In 1889, at the Universal Exhibition in Paris, the jewelry firms of Vever and Boucheron included collaborative works by Lalique in their displays.

In the early 1890s, Lalique began to incorporate glass into his jewelry, and in 1893 he took part in a competition organized by the Union Centrale des Arts Decoratifs to design a drinking vessel. He won second prize.

Lalique opened his first Paris retail shop in 1905, near the perfume business of François Coty. Coty commissioned Lalique to design his perfume labels in 1907, and he also created his first perfume bottles for Coty.

In the first decade of the 20th century, Lalique continued to experiment with glass manufacturing techniques, and mounted his first show devoted entirely to glass in 1911.

During World War I, Lalique's first factory was forced to close, but the construction of a new factory was soon begun in Wingen-sur-Moder, in the Alsace region. It was completed in 1921, and still produces Lalique crystal today.

In 1925, Lalique designed the first "car mascot" (bouchons de radiateur, or hood ornament) for Citroën, the French automobile company. For the next six years, Lalique would design 29 models for companies such as Bentley, Bugatti, Delage, Hispano-Suiza, Rolls Royce, and Voisin.

Lalique's second boutique opened in 1931, and this location continues to serve as the main Lalique showroom today.

René Lalique died on May 5, 1945, at the age of 85. His son, Marc, took over the business at that time, and when Marc died in 1977, his daughter, Marie-Claude Lalique Dedouvre, assumed control of the company. She sold her interest in the firm and retired in 1994. She died on April 14, 2003, at the age of 67.

On the Cover: Lalique vase Esna was released in 1985 to mark the 125th anniversary of René Lalique's birth. Esna was named for a temple from the time of Ptolemy rediscovered on the Nile. It was inspired by a voyage to Egypt by Marie-Claude Lalique, then president and exclusive designer of Cristal Lalique. The 9" vase is valued at $1,500-$2,000.

Tips for Collectors

Color: Examples of colored Lalique glass are the most sought-after, with intense colors being among the most highly prized. (The exception to this rule is deep purple or amethyst, which may be is an indication that a clear piece of glass has been irradiated.) Also, pieces with rich opalescent color, enameled details, or applied patina that has remained strong in color, are often valued more than pieces in clear and frosted glass.

Crispness: The details in mold patterns get worn over time, so look for pieces with well-defined features and crisp edges on design elements.

Cire-Perdue: The surface of Lalique glass made with this lost-wax process may appear opaque, rough and grainy (some even bear fingerprints), and have applied patination, often sepia. These are the rarest of all Lalique glass items, and only a few hundred are thought to exist.

Marks: Early pieces are often marked "R. Lalique" or "R. Lalique, France," either stenciled, molded, or engraved. After Rene Lalique's death in 1945, the "Lalique, France" (with no R) mark appeared, sometimes with mold numbers. Carefully examine pieces with hand-engraved marks, and consult with an experienced dealer in Lalique to pick out forgeries.

Repairs: Check for signs of grinding or excessive polishing around the necks and bases of Lalique vases, and on pieces whose intended uses contributed to damage, like tableware, ashtrays, perfume containers, letter seals, and inkwells.

Prices

The prices in this book have been compiled from auction records, collector valuations and the resources of respected dealers in Lalique. Like any collecting area, values reflect rarity, condition, changes in taste, and the wider economy. The adage that "an antique is worth what someone will pay for it" holds true for Lalique glass, and the prices found here are only a guide. A price guide measures not only current values, but also captures a moment in time, and sometimes that moment may pass very quickly. Collectors should consult experienced, qualified resources when trying to determine values.

The Big Book

In the descriptions of Lalique pieces that follow, you will find notations like this: "M p. 478, No. 1100." This refers to the page and serial numbers found in *René Lalique, maître-verrier, 1860-1945: Analyse de L'oeuvre et Catalogue Raisonné, by Félix Marcilhac, published in 1989 and revised in 1994.*

Printed entirely in French, this book of more than 1,000 pages is the definitive guide to Lalique's work, and listings from auction catalogs typically cite the Marcilhac guide as a reference. A used copy can cost more than $500. Copies in any condition are extremely difficult to find, but collectors consider Marcilhac's guide to be the bible for Lalique.

Ashtrays

Vintage Lalique ashtrays remain some of the most affordable examples of the company's pre-1945 production. Like dinnerware, the nature of their use contributes to damage, so be aware of areas that have been highly polished in an attempt to remove signs of chipping.

"Alice"
circa 1924, in clear and frosted glass, molded R.LALIQUE, stenciled R. LALIQUE FRANCE, 4 1/3" long. (M p. 272, No. 289)

$450-$500

"Anthenor"
in clear and frosted glass, circa 1927, 5 1/2" diameter. (M p. 273, No. 293)

$500+

"Archers"
in deep red glass, circa 1922, 5 1/2" diameter. (M p. 269, No. 278)

$2,500+

"Archers"
in black glass, circa 1922, 5 1/2" diameter. (M p. 269, No. 278)

$1,200+

"Archers"
in clear and frosted glass, circa 1922, 5 1/2" diameter. (M p. 269, No. 278)

$700+

"Canard"
circa 1925, in opalescent, yellow and green glass, engraved R. Lalique France, No. 283, 3" tall. (M p. 270, No. 283)

$700-$800 each

"Berthe"
in satin glass, circa 1929, 3" diameter. (M p. 276, No. 302)

$600+

"Caravelle"
in clear and frosted glass, circa 1930, 4 3/4" diameter. (M p. 279, No. 312)

$350+

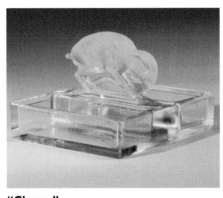

"Chevre"
a double ashtray or cigarette holder, circa 1936, in clear and frosted glass, stenciled R. LALIQUE, 5 1/8" diameter. (M p. 283, No. 333)

$450-$550

"Caravelle"
in opalescent glass, circa 1930, 4 3/4 diameter. (M p. 279, No. 312)

$450+

"Chien"
in opalescent green glass, engraved R. Lalique France No. 290, 3 7/8" tall. (Ref. M p. 272, No. 290)

$550-$650

"Chien"
in topaz glass with gray patina, circa 1926, Engraved R. Lalique, 3 5/8" tall. (M p. 272)

$325-$375

"Chien"
in clear and frosted glass, circa 1926, engraved R. Lalique, 3 5/8" tall. (M p. 272, No. 290)

$325-$375

"Cuba"
in deep amber glass, wheel-cut R. LALIQUE FRANCE. (Ref. M p. 273, No. 294.)

$900-$1,100

"Chien"
in amber glass, circa 1926, engraved R. Lalique, 3 5/8" tall. (M p. 272, No. 290)

$325-$375

"Deux Colombes"
in clear and frosted glass, circa 1931, 4 3/4" diameter. (M p. 280, No. 320)

$250+

"Dindon"
circa 1925, in topaz glass, stenciled R. LALIQUE FRANCE, 3" tall. (M p. 272, No. 287)

$350-$450

"Deux Zephyrs"
in amber glass, circa 1913, 3 1/8" diameter. (M p. 269, No. 275)

$400+

"Deux Zephyrs"
in clear and frosted glass, circa 1913, 3 1/8" diameter. (M p. 269, No. 275)

$250+

"Dindon"
circa 1925, in amber glass with gray patina, engraved R. Lalique France, 3" tall. (M p. 272, No. 287)

$375-$425

"Ecureuil"
in amber glass, circa 1931, 4 3/4" diameter. (M p. 279, No. 315)

$500+

Ashtrays

"Fauvettes"
circa 1924, in red glass, stenciled LALIQUE FRANCE, 6 7/8" diameter. (M p. 270, No. 282)

$500+

"Fauvettes"
circa 1924, in clear and frosted glass with sepia patina, stenciled LALIQUE FRANCE, 6 7/8" diameter. (M p. 270, No. 282)

$275-$325

"Fauvettes"
circa 1924, in opalescent glass with blue patina, stenciled LALIQUE FRANCE, 6 7/8" diameter. (M p. 270, No. 282)

$275-$325

"Feuilles"
circa 1934, in amber glass, engraved R. Lalique, edge reduced by polishing, 6 1/2" long. (M p. 270, No. 279)

$90-$110

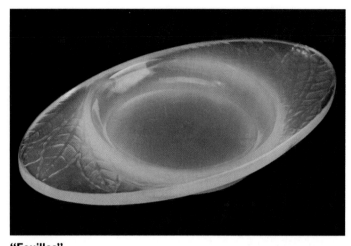

"Feuilles"
circa 1934, in opalescent glass, engraved R. Lalique No. 279, 6 1/2" long. (M p. 270, No. 279)

$275-$325

"Feuilles"
in amber glass, circa 1924, engraved R. Lalique, 6 5/8" long. (M p. 270, No. 279)

$350+

"Feuilles"
in cased red glass, circa 1924, engraved R. Lalique, 6 5/8" long. (M p. 270, No. 279)

$600+

Ashtrays

"Irene"
"Irene" in clear and frosted glass, circa 1929, stenciled R. LALIQUE FRANCE, 3 3/4" diameter. (M p. 276, No. 304)

$500+

"Irene"
in deep green glass, circa 1929, stenciled R. LALIQUE FRANCE, 3 3/4" diameter. (M p. 276, No. 304)

$1,200-$1,500

"Lapin"
in topaz glass, engraved R. Lalique France. (Ref. M p. 271, No. 285.)

$550-$650

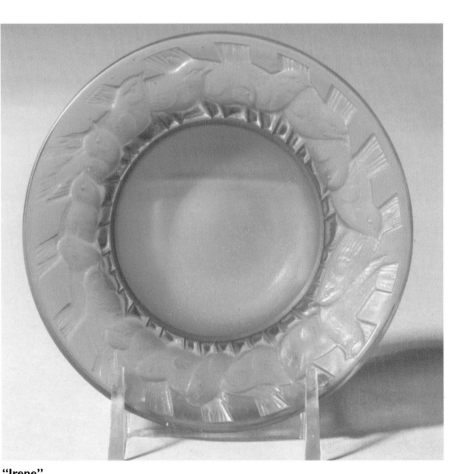

"Jeanne Lanvin"
in clear and frosted glass, circa 1925, 4 1/8" tall. (M p. 267, B)

$500+

"Irene"
in bright green glass, stenciled R. LALIQUE FRANCE. (Ref. M p. 276, No. 304.)

$1,200-$1,500

"Louise"
in satin glass, circa 1929, 3" diameter. (M p. 275, No. 301)

$600+

"Martinique"
circa 1928, in deep amber glass, wheel-cut R. LALIQUE FRANCE, 6" long. (M p. 274, No. 298)

$900-$1,000

"Medicis"
circa 1924, in opalescent glass, molded R. LALIQUE, 5 3/4" long. (M p. 270, No. 280)

$550-$650

"Moineau"
in yellow glass, circa 1925, 4 3/4" diameter. (M p. 271, No. 284)

$800+

"Medicis"
in blue glass, circa 1924, molded R. LALIQUE, 5 3/4" long. (M p. 270, No. 280)

$1,500-$1,600

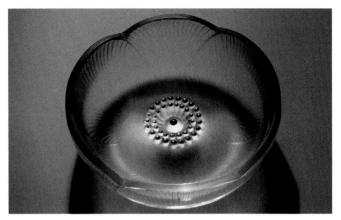

"Nicole"
in satin glass, circa 1929, 3 3/8" diameter. (M p. 277, No. 304)

$400+

"Renard"
in amber glass, circa 1926, 4 3/4" diameter. (M p. 272, No. 291)

$600+

"Paquerette"
circa 1929, in clear and frosted glass with black enameled detail, stenciled R. LALIQUE, engraved France, 3 1/8" diameter. (M p. 275, No. 299)

$250-$300

"Renard"
in topaz glass, circa 1926, 4 3/4" diameter. (M p. 272, No. 291)

$450+

"Rapace"
in clear and frosted glass, circa 1931, 4 3/4" diameter. (M p. 281, No. 323)

$350+

"Sirenes"
in amber glass, circa 1920, 4 1/2" diameter. (M p. 269, No. 277)

$450+

"Souris"
in clear and frosted glass, circa 1925, 4 3/4" diameter. (M p. 271, No. 286)

$350+

"Serpent"
in clear and frosted glass, circa 1920, 4 1/2" diameter. (M p. 269, No. 276)

$300+

"Souris"
in topaz glass, circa 1925, 4 3/4" diameter. (M p. 271, No. 286)

$500+

"Statuette de la Fontaine"
in clear and frosted glass, circa 1925, 4 1/2" tall. (M p. 272, No. 288)

$900+

Ashtrays

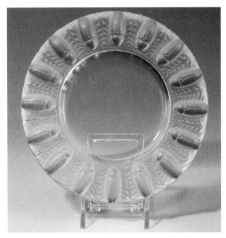

"Tobago"
designed 1928, this example circa 1960, in clear and frosted glass, molded R. LALIQUE, 5 1/2" diameter. (M p. 273, No. 295)

$200-$250

"Vezelay"
circa 1928, in clear and frosted glass with blue patina, molded R. LALIQUE, 4 1/2" diameter. (M p. 270, No. 281)

$225-$275

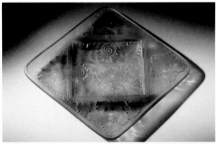

"Vezelay"
circa 1928, in green glass, molded R. LALIQUE and engraved R. Lalique France No. 281, 4 1/2" diameter. (M p. 270, No. 281)

$200-$300

"Tobago"
in deep amber glass, circa 1928, 5 1/2" diameter. (M p. 273, No. 295)

$400+

"Vezelay"
circa 1928, in deep amber glass, molded R. LALIQUE and engraved R. Lalique France No. 481, 4 1/2" diameter. (M p. 270, No. 281)

$300-$400

"Vezelay"
circa 1928, in clear and frosted glass, molded R.
LALIQUE and engraved R. Lalique France No. 281,
4 1/2" diameter. (M p. 270, No. 281)
$200-$300

Groups of Modern Ashtrays

Two ashtrays
circa 1970, "Bluets," 5 3/4" long, and a commemorative ashtray in "Honfleur"
pattern for Linz Jewelers of Dallas, Texas, 5 1/2" diameter.
$125-$175/pair

Three clear glass ashtrays
Engraved Lalique France. Average diameter 4".
$200-$250

Four clear glass ashtrays
Engraved Lalique France. Average diameter 3 1/2".
$300-$350/set

Three ashtrays
circa 1970, a pair of cigar ashtrays in "Santa Maria" pattern, and a "Caravelle" cigarette ashtray, largest 6
3/4" diameter.
$325-$425/set

Ashtrays

Four clear glass ashtrays
Engraved Lalique France. Average diameter 4 3/4".

$275-$325/set

Two ashtrays
including "Tokio," with a matching cigarette holder, engraved Lalique France. Average diameter 5 1/8".

$250-$300/pair

Three ashtrays
circa 1970, together with "Goujon," figure of a leaping fish, all engraved Lalique France, largest 6" diameter.

$125-$175/set

Three ashtrays
all circa 1970, in clear and frosted glass, various designs, all engraved Lalique France.

$150-$200/set

Three ashtrays
circa 1970, all engraved Lalique France. Average 4" diameter.

$125-$175/set

Bowls

Prices for decorative Lalique bowls (as opposed to those used as part of a table service) have been rising steadily in recent years, with prices ranging from around $400 to $4,000 for a pristine example of "Perruches" from the early 1930s, in opalescent glass with blue patina.

"Bulbes"
circa 1935, in opalescent glass, stenciled R. LALIQUE FRANCE, 8 1/8" diameter. (M p. 763, No. 3300)

$400-$500

"Calypso"
shallow bowl, opalescent glass, circa 1930, 14 1/2" diameter. (M p. 301, No. 413)

$1,200+

Bowls

"Coquilles"
a group of three opalescent bowls, circa 1924, in graduated size, all wheel-cut R. LALIQUE FRANCE with design Nos. 3200, 3201, 3202, 9 1/2", 8 1/4", 7 1/4" diameter.. (M p. 701, Nos. 3200, 3201, 3202)

$900-$1,100/set

"Coquilles No.2"
a bowl, circa 1924, in opalescent glass, molded R. LALIQUE, engraved France, 8 1/4" diameter. (M p.748, No. 3201)

$550-$650

"Chiens"
circa 1921, in opalescent glass, molded R. Lalique, engraved France, 9 1/2" diameter. (M p. 749, No. 3214)

$900-$1,000

"Fleur"
circa 1912, in clear and frosted glass with sepia patina and black enamel, molded R. LALIQUE, 4 1/2" diameter. (M p. 727, No. 3100)

$650-$750

"Fleurons"
circa 1935, in opalescent glass, stenciled R. LALIQUE FRANCE, 8 1/8" diameter. (M p. 765, No. 3312)

$500-$600

"Dauphins"
circa 1932, in opalescent glass, stenciled R. LALIQUE, 9 1/3" diameter. (M p. 307, No. 10-384)

$700-$800

"Floride"
clear and green glass with black enamel details, circa 1960, engraved Lalique France, 7 1/4" diameter.

$300-$350

"Gui"
circa 1921, in opalescent glass, stenciled R. LALIQUE FRANCE, 8 1/8" diameter. (M p. 751, No. 3224)

$450-$525

"Marguerites"
a center bowl, circa 1941, in clear and frosted glass with green patina, stenciled R. LALIQUE FRANCE, 4 3/4" diameter. (M p. 312, No. 10-404)

$900-$1,000

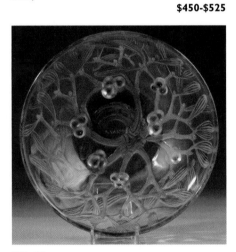

"Gui"
circa 1921, in clear and frosted glass with sepia patina, stenciled R. LALIQUE FRANCE, 8 1/8" diameter. (M p. 751, No. 3224)

$450-$525

"Molsheim"
a bowl, in clear and frosted glass, circa 1931, 4 1/2" diameter. (M p. 730, No. 3119)

$200+

"Nemours"
designed in 1929, this example circa 1970, in clear and frosted glass with black enamel highlights, 9 3/4" diameter. (M p. 299, No. 404)

$400-$550

"Ondes"
circa 1935, in opalescent glass, stenciled R. LALIQUE FRANCE, 8 1/8" diameter. (M p. 762, No. 3292)

$350-$450

"Nemours"
circa 1929, in clear and frosted glass with sepia patina and brown enameled highlights, molded R. LALIQUE FRANCE, 10" diameter. (M p. 299, No. 404)

$900-$1,000

Bowls

"Ondines"
circa 1921, in clear and frosted glass with blue patina, engraved R. Lalique France, 8 1/4" diameter. (M p. 292, No. 380)

$700-$800

"Pinsons"
a modern bowl, together with "Nogent," a modern vase, both engraved Lalique France, bowl 9 1/4" diameter.

$350-$400/pair

"Ondines"
circa 1921, in opalescent glass, wheel-cut R. LALIQUE FRANCE, 8 1/2" diameter. (M p. 699, No. 3003)

$1,200-$1,500

"Pinsons"
designed 1933, this example circa 1940, in clear and frosted glass with sepia patina, engraved Lalique, 9 1/8" diameter. (M p. 307, No. 10-386)

$550-$650

"Perruches"
circa 1931, in opalescent glass with blue patina, stenciled R. LALIQUE FRANCE, 9 5/8" diameter. (M p. 302, No. 419)

$4,000-$4,500

"Poissons"
circa 1921, in opalescent glass, 9 3/8" diameter. (M p. 749, No. 3211)

$750-$850

"Volubilis"
circa 1921, in yellow opalescent glass, wheel-cut R. LALIQUE FRANCE, 8 1/2" diameter. (M p. 293, No. 383)

$650-$750

"Tournon"
a center bowl, circa 1928, in opalescent glass, molded R. LALIQUE FRANCE, 12" diameter. (M p. 298, No. 401)

$1,100-$1,400

Boxes

Included in this section are cigarette and powder boxes, and examples made with wood, celluloid, and aluminum. Sizes range from tiny containers, barely 2" square, to a large wood "coffret" more than 12" long.

"Cerises"
circa 1923, in black celluloid, molded R. LALIQUE, 2 3/4" square. (M p. 236, No. 72)

$800-$900

"Cerises"
circa 1923, in red celluloid, molded R. LALIQUE, 2 1/8" square. (M p. 236, No. 73)

$900-$1,100

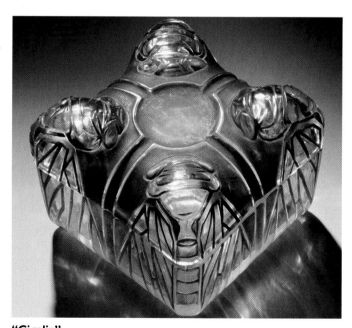

"Cheveux de Venus"
in topaz glass, circa 1910, 2 1/5" diameter. (M p. 234, No. 63)

$1,500+

"Cigalia"
a powder box for Roger et Gallet, in clear and frosted glass with charcoal patina, circa 1924, 3" square. (M p. 970, Roger et Gallet 2)

$600+

"Clematite"
a powder box for Coty, in clear and frosted glass, circa 1911, 2 1/2" diameter. (M p. 967, Coty 2)

$500+

"Coq"
in black glass with white patina, circa 1910, 4" diameter. (M p. 223, No. 2)

$600+

"Cleones"
circa 1921, in opalescent glass, molded R. LALIQUE, engraved France, 6 3/4" diameter. (M p. 231, No. 49)

$800-$1,000

"Coquilles"
in electric blue glass, circa 1920, 2 3/4" diameter. (M p. 236, No. 71)

$1,500+

"Cleones"
circa 1921, in amber glass, molded R. LALIQUE, engraved France, 6 3/4" diameter. (M p. 231, No. 9)

$900-$1,100

"Copellia"
circa 1960, in clear and frosted glass, the hinged cover with gilt metal mounts, engraved Lalique France, 6 3/4" long. (M p. 223, No. 4, original version)

$400-$450

Boxes

"Dans La Nuit"
a powder box for Worth, in clear and frosted glass with blue patina, circa 1926; in two sizes, 5" and 5 1/2" tall. (M p. 971, Worth 1)

$900-$1,200

"Degas"
in clear and frosted glass with gray patina, molded LALIQUE. (Ref. M p. 235, No. 66)

$1,200-$1,500

"Degas"
in satin glass, circa 1921, 3 1/8" diameter. (M p. 235, No. 66)

$1,500+

"Deux Sirenes"
in amber glass, circa 1921, 10" diameter. (M p. 230, No. 43)

$3,000+

"D'Orsay 2"
a powder box for D'Orsay, in opalescent glass and card, with original silk packaged face powder, circa 1920, molded R. LALIQUE, 3 1/3" diameter. (M p. 968, D'Orsay 2)

$1,000-$1,200

"Eglantines"
circa 1926, in clear and frosted glass with blue patina, engraved R. Lalique France, 5 1/3" diameter. (M p. 241, No. 94)

$600-$700

"Enfants"
a powder box, circa 1931, in clear and frosted glass with sepia patina, engraved R. Lalique, 4 1/4" diameter. (M p. 345, No. 610)

$400-$500

"Emiliane"
circa 1920, in clear and frosted glass, engraved R. Lalique France, 3 1/2" diameter. (M p. 235, No. 70)

$300-$350

"Fleurs D'Amour"
a powder box and compact for Roger et Gallet, in aluminum with sepia patina, unopened and in original card box, together with a factice card box for Pavots d'Argent by Roger et Gallet. Both signed. (M p. 970, No.3)

$250-$350/pair

"Enfants"
in clear and frosted glass, and a matching perfume bottle, both circa 1970 (designed 1931), both engraved Lalique France, 3 1/4" and 4" tall. (M p. 345, Nos. 609 and 610, original version)

$300-$350/pair

"Fleurs D'Amour"
a powder box for Roger et Gallet, in aluminum with red patina, with original face powder, signed, 3" diameter. (M p. 970, No. 3)

$200-$250/pair

Boxes

"Fleurs D'Amour"
a powder box for Roger et Gallet, in aluminum,
signed, 3" diameter. (M p. 970, Roger et Gallet 3)

$150+

"Fleurs D'Amour"
a powder box for Roger et Gallet, in aluminum with
sepia patina, signed, 3" diameter. (M p. 970, No. 3)

$150-$200

"Fontainebleau"
circa 1921, in clear and frosted glass with gray
patina, molded R. LALIQUE, 3 1/3" diameter. (M p.
233, No. 59)

$500-$600

"Gui"
in clear and frosted glass, circa 1910, 4" diameter.
(M p. 234, No. 65)

$350+

"Georgette"
circa 1922, in opalescent glass with satin and card base, molded R. LALIQUE, 8 1/4" diameter. (M p. 30, No. 45)

$1,700-$2,000

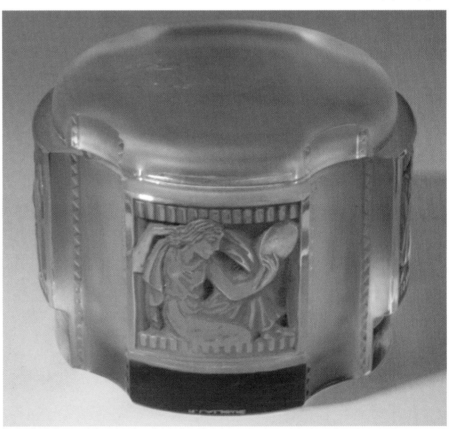

"Helene"
a powder box, circa 1942, in clear and frosted glass with sepia patina, stenciled R. LALIQUE, 4 1/2" diameter.
(M p. 348, No. 635)

$400-$450

"Hirondelles"
a cigarette box, circa 1923, in clear and frosted glass, 4" long. (M p. 222, No. 53)

$550-$650

"Le Lys"
a powder box for D'Orsay, circa 1922, in clear and frosted glass with sepia patina, molded R. LALIQUE FRANCE, 3 3/8" diameter. (M p. 968, No. 3)

$250-$300

"Le Lys"
a powder box for D'Orsay, circa 1922, in clear and frosted glass, molded R. LALIQUE FRANCE (M p. 968, No. 3), together with an aluminum powder box for Coty, 3 3/8" diameter.

$275-$325/pair

"L'Origan"
a powder box for Coty, in clear and frosted glass with strong sepia patina, circa 1912, 3 1/2" diameter. (M p. 967, Coty 3)

$350+

"Le Lys"
a powder box and cover for D'Orsay, in clear and frosted glass, with original goose down powder puff and card packaging, molded R. LALIQUE FRANCE, 3 3/8" diameter. (M p. 168, No. 3)

$350-$400

"Le Lys"
a powder box and cover for D'Orsay, in clear and frosted glass, with strong sepia patina, 3 1/3" diameter. (M p. 968, D'Orsay 3)

$300+

"Marguerites"
a powder box for Houbigant, in clear and frosted glass with gray patina, circa 1926, 2 1/3" tall. (M p. 970, Houbigant 3)

$250+

Boxes

"Louveciennes"
circa 1910, in clear and frosted glass, molded LALIQUE DEPOSE, 2 3/4"
diameter. (M p. 223, No. 5)

$1,800-$2,200

"Mesanges"
circa 1921, in opalescent amber glass, molded R.LALIQUE, 6 3/4" diameter. (M p
232, No. 52)

$900-$1,100

"Monnaie Du Pape"
a wood "coffret" (casket or box), circa 1920, the cover with a single mirrored panel, in clear and frosted glass with sepia patina, wheel-cut R. LALIQUE, 3 3/8" by 12
1/8" by 7 1/2".

$6,000-$8,000

"Primeveres"
circa 1930, in opalescent glass, molded R. LALIQUE, 7 7/8" diameter. (M p. 239, No. 86)

$900-$1,000

"Quatre Parfums D'Orsay"
a powder box for D'Orsay, in black glass with white patina, circa 1927, 7 7/8" square. (M p. 968, D'Orsay 5)

$1,500+

"Quatre Papillons"
in opalescent glass with gray patina, circa 1911, 3 1/8 in. diameter. (M p. 225, No. 14)

$1,200+

"Quatre Papillons"
in clear and frosted glass with strong sepia patina, circa 1911, 3 1/8" diameter. (M p. 225, No. 14)

$1,200+

"Quatre Scarabees"
in cobalt blue glass with white patina, circa 1911, engraved R. Lalique France, No.15, 3 3/8" diameter. (M p. 225, No. 15)

$2,500-$2,800

Boxes

"Quatre Scarabees"
circa 1911, in black glass with white patina, engraved R. Lalique France, No. 15, 3 3/8" diameter. (M p. 225, No. 15)

$2,500-$2,800

"Roger"
in clear and frosted glass, circa 1926, 5 1/3" diameter. (M p. 237, No. 75)

$400+

"Quatre Scarabees"
in teal green glass, circa 1911, engraved R. Lalique France, No. 15, 3 3/8" diameter. (M p. 225, No. 15)

$2,500-$2,800

"Roger"
circa 1926, in topaz glass, molded LALIQUE, 5 1/4" diameter. (M p. 237, No. 75)

$600-$650

"Scarabee"
a powder box for Piver, in black glass with white patina and strong mold, circa 1911, 3 1/2" diameter. (M p. 970, Piver 1)

$2,000+

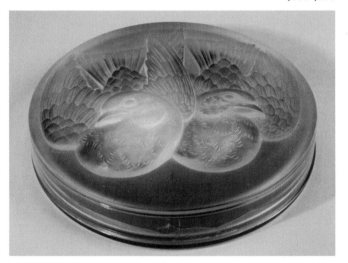

"Saint-Marc"
circa 1922, in opalescent glass, molded R. LALIQUE, 9 7/8" diameter. (M p. 238, No. 81)

$1,500-$1,800

"Saint Nectaire"
circa 1925, in clear and frosted glass with green patina, engraved R. Lalique France, 3 3/8" diameter. (M p. 237, No. 76)

$500-$600

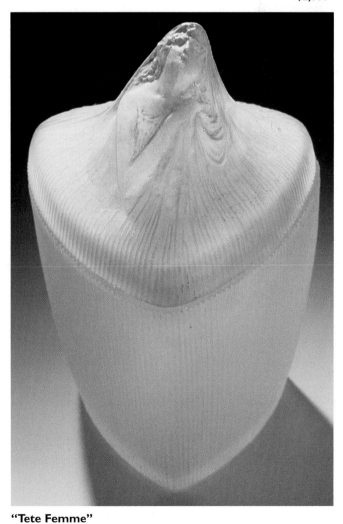

"Tete Femme"
a powder box for Coty, in satin glass with traces of sepia patina, circa 1912, 3 3/4" tall. (M p. 967, Coty 4)

$2,500+

Boxes

"Trois Figurines"
a powder box for D'Orsay, circa 1912, in clear and frosted glass, molded R. LALIQUE, 3 5/8" tall. (M p. 968, No. 1); together with "Fleurettes," a sponge bowl, circa 1923, in clear and frosted glass, engraved R. Lalique France, 7 1/8" diameter. (M p. 342, No. 984)

$175-$225/pair

Two powder boxes for D'Orsay
circa 1920, in clear and frosted glass, comprising "Le Lys" and "Trois Figurines." Both molded R. LALIQUE. (M p. 968, Nos. 1 and 3.)

$400-$450/pair

"Trois Figurines"
a powder box for D'Orsay, in clear and frosted glass with strong sepia patina, circa 1912, 3 3/4" diameter. (M p. 968, D'Orsay 1)

$200+

"Vallauris"
circa 1928, in clear and frosted glass, engraved R. Lalique France, 5 1/2" diameter. (M p. 239, No. 84)

$300-$350

Four powder boxes
circa 1920-25, comprising "Trois Figurines" for D'Orsay in clear and frosted glass, containing a silk wrapped powder, together with three aluminum boxes for Roger et Gallet in "Fleur D'Amour" pattern. All with molded signatures, 3 3/4" and 3" diameter. (M p. 968 and 970.)

$250-$300/set

Car Mascots
(Hood Ornaments)

René Lalique was always experimenting, producing vases, statues, dinnerware, etc. He added car mascots ("bouchons de radiateur") to his production in the late 1920s.

The popularity of the car mascots was such that Lalique commissioned the Breves Gallery in Knightsbridge, London, to supply metal mounts to British customers, and the Breves name was placed on the side of the mounting. Breves had the world rights to market Lalique mascots.

Though the range of car mascots numbers 27 in the 1932 Lalique catalogue, Breves gallery offered the Small Mermaid in its own catalogues as a car mascot, and also is believed to have offered the larger Mermaid, making a total of 29 in all. The first Lalique mascot was commissioned by the Citroen company in 1925, the "5 horses," for the model 5CV. There followed 27 more, depicting horse heads, various bird and animal forms, nude figures, and even a shooting star.

Only one mascot was produced in two versions: the horse's head, Longchamps. The other horse's head, Epsom, has a pronounced forward thrust.

The rarest production mascot is certainly the fox, with only a few known examples surviving. The most famous and largest is the "Victoire" or "Spirit of the Wind."

The Lalique factory still produces seven paperweights today, which were originally made as car mascots: Chrysis, eagle's head, small cock, boar, perch, St. Christopher, and the cock's head.

Contemporary copies of Lalique car mascots have been made in the U.S., but these often appear yellow in tinge and usually have factory relief molded markings around the top lip of the base. Czechoslovakian copies also exist in inferior frosted glass but with no signatures.

Usually these pieces are found glued to black square marble bases. These pieces have also been found polished to the clear glass, and with a spurious etched R. Lalique signature.

In recent years, a few deep purple glass pieces have appeared on the market. Genuine clear examples have been irradiated recently to achieve this effect. Great caution and expert help should be sought when these are offered for sale to determine their validity.

— Tony Wraight, of Finesse Fine Art, Dorset, U.K.

"Archer"
in clear and frosted glass, wheel-cut R. LALIQUE FRANCE. (M p. 498, No. 1126)

$3,000-$3,500

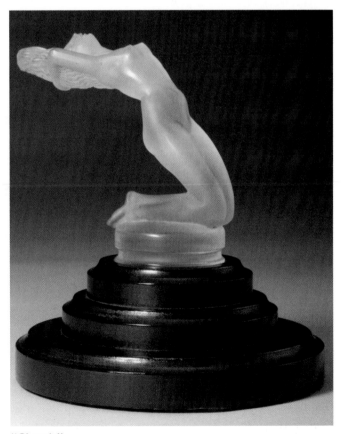

"Chrysis"
in clear and frosted glass with sepia patina, stenciled R. LALIQUE, with an ebonized wood display stand. (M p. 505, No. 1183.)

$5,000-$6,000

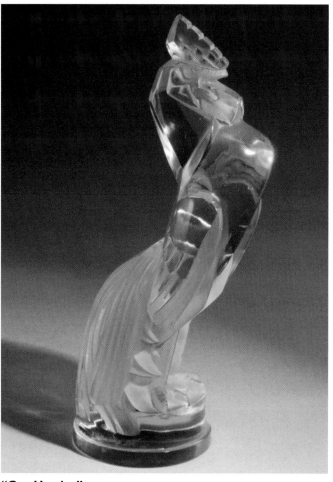

"Coq Houdan"
circa 1929, in clear and frosted glass, wheel-cut R. LALIQUE FRANCE, 8" tall. (M p. 504, No. 1161)

$4,000-$5,000

"Faucon"
circa 1925, in clear and frosted glass, molded R. LALIQUE, wheel-cut FRANCE, 6" tall. (M p. 298, No. 1124)

$2,800-$3,300

"Coq Nain"
circa 1928, in clear and frosted glass, molded R. LALIQUE FRANCE, 8 1/8" tall. (M p. 498, No. 1135)

$800-$1,000

"Faucon"
circa 1925, in clear and frosted glass, molded R. LALIQUE, wheel-cut FRANCE, 4 1/2" tall. (M p. 498, No. 1124)

$2,500-$3,000

"Hirondelle"
circa 1928, in clear and frosted glass, molded R. LALIQUE FRANCE, 6" tall. (M p. 501, No. 1143)

$1,500-$2,000

"Libellule"
Grande Modele, circa 1928, in clear and frosted glass with amethyst tint, molded R. LALIQUE FRANCE and engraved R. Lalique France, 8 1/4" tall, large chip to foot. (M p. 501, No. 1145)

$2,800-$3,300

"Perche"
designed 1929, this example circa 1950, in clear and frosted glass with blue patina, molded R. LALIQUE, 6" long. (M p. 503, No. 1158)

$1,200-$1,400

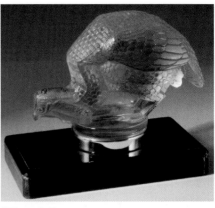

"Pintade"
circa 1929, in clear and frosted glass, with original chrome collar, molded R. LALIQUE, 6" long. (M p. 504, No. 1164)

$4,000-$5,000

"Libellule"
Grande Modele, circa 1928, in clear and frosted glass with pale amethyst tint, molded R. LALIQUE FRANCE and engraved R. Lalique France, 8 1/4" tall, accompanied by a letter authenticating the mascot as the one formerly used by Gary Cooper on his Duesenberg, and presented by Cooper as a gift. (M p. 501, No. 1145)

$9,000-$12,000

"Sainte-Christophe"
circa 1928, this example circa 1985, in clear and frosted glass, molded LALIQUE FRANCE, 4 1/2" tall. (M p. 501, No. 1142)

$700-$800

"Sainte-Christophe"
circa 1928, in clear and frosted glass with amethyst tint, molded R. LALIQUE FRANCE, 5 1/8" tall. (M p. 501, No. 1142)

$650-$750

"Sainte-Christophe"
circa 1928, in clear and frosted glass, molded R. LALIQUE FRANCE, 5 1/8" tall. (M p. 501, No. 1142)

$900-$1,100

"Sainte-Christophe"
a hood ornament, in clear and frosted glass with gray patina, molded R. Lalique, with a Lalique-style chrome display stand. (M p. 501, No. 1142)

$1,200-$1,500

"Sanglier"
circa 1929, in topaz glass, molded R. LALIQUE, and stenciled R. LALIQUE FRANCE, 3 5/8" long. (M p. 503, No. 1157)

$900-$1,100

"Sirene"
circa 1920, in clear and frosted glass, molded R. LALIQUE, engraved R. Lalique France, 3 3/4" tall. (M p. 497, No. 831)

$2,800-$3,200

"Tete D'Aigle"
designed in 1928, this example circa 1960, in clear
and frosted glass, molded R. LALIQUE FRANCE,
engraved Lalique France, 4 1/4" tall. (M p. 499, No.
1138)

$550-$650

"Tete D'Aigle"
circa 1928, in collar and onyx base. (M p. 499,
No. 1138)

$2,000-$2,500

"Tete D'Aigle"
a modern hood ornament, designed circa 1928, in
clear and frosted glass, engraved Lalique France, 4"
tall.

$200-$250

"Tete de Coq"
designed in 1928, this example circa 1950, in clear
and frosted glass, molded LALIQUE FRANCE, 7"
tall. (M p. 499, No. 1137)

$550-$650

"Tete de Coq"
circa 1928, in clear and frosted glass, molded
LALIQUE FRANCE, 6 7/8" tall. (M p. 499, No. 1137)

$1,000-$1,200

"Tete de Paon"
circa 1928, in clear and frosted glass, molded R.
LALIQUE FRANCE, comb missing, 4 3/4" tall. (M p.
500, No. 1140)

$500-$700

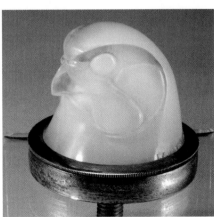

"Tete D'Epervier"
circa 1928, in opalescent glass, with original
chrome collar, molded LALIQUE FRANCE, 2
1/2" tall. (M p. 499, No. 1139)

$2,500-$2,800

Car Mascots

Three automobile hood ornaments
in clear and frosted glass, designed in the late 1920s, these examples circa 1980, comprising "Coq Nain," "Perche," and "Chrysis." Modern marks, tallest 8".

$500-$600/set

"Victoire"
1938, in amethyst-tinted glass, molded R. LALIQUE FRANCE, 10" long. (M p. 502, No. 1147)

$20,000-$23,000

"Victoire"
circa 1928, in clear and frosted glass, molded R. LALIQUE FRANCE, 10 1/4" long, together with an original Lalique wood display mount. (M p. 502, No. 1147)

$24,000-$26,000

Cire Perdue

The surface of Lalique glass made with this lost-wax process may appear opaque, rough and grainy (some even bear fingerprints), and have applied patination, often sepia. These are the rarest of all Lalique glass items, and only a few hundred are thought to exist.

"Cenotaphe, Couvercle Roses"
vase, cire perdue glass, circa 1923, 6 1/3" tall. (M p. 1051, No. CP 521)

No Established Value

"Quatre Feuilles Composees Formant Angles"
vase, cire perdue glass, circa 1923, 3 1/4" tall. (M p. 1047, No. CP 498)

No Established Value

"Satyre Avec Pied Petit Faune Dormant"

No Established Value

"Tigre au Rocher sur un Chapiteau Gothique"
statuette, cire perdue glass, circa 1919, 6" tall. (M p. 1001, No. CP 135)

No Established Value

Figures

Early Lalique figures are among the rarest examples of the company's production. Some are actually models for larger works, while others were intended to be illuminated decorations. Note the price difference for the statuettes called "Suzanne" from the mid-1920s. Both are made of opalescent glass, but the example with the original bronze illuminating stand commands double the price of the figure without a stand.

Three figures of birds
circa 1970-1980, in clear and frosted glass, comprising seagull, sparrow, and swallow bookend, various Lalique France marks, tallest 9".

$350-$400/set

Four figurines
circa 1980, in clear and frosted glass, comprising "Leda," "Floreal" with black glass base, and a pair of "Faune" groups. Various marks, tallest 5 1/2". (Lalique design Nos. 1190500, 1190700, and 1191599)

$600-$700/set

Three figurines
circa 1970, in clear and frosted glass, comprising "Leda," "Diane," and "Floreal," with black glass base. All engraved Lalique France.

$250-$300/set

"Chat Assis"
a figure of a sitting cat, circa 1970, in clear and frosted glass, engraved Lalique France, 8 1/4" tall.

$650-$750

"Coq De Jungle"
a decorative sculpture, circa 1936, in clear and frosted glass, stenciled R. LALIQUE FRANCE, signature obscured by polishing, 16" tall. (M p. 493, No. 1124)

$1,500-$1,800

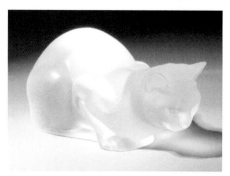

"Chat Couche"
a figure of a crouching cat, circa 1970, in clear and frosted glass, engraved Lalique France, 9 1/4" long.

$550-$650

Figure of a woman

with flowers, circa 1905, cire-perdue glass with charcoal patina, 18" tall not including base, one of only three known.

No established value.

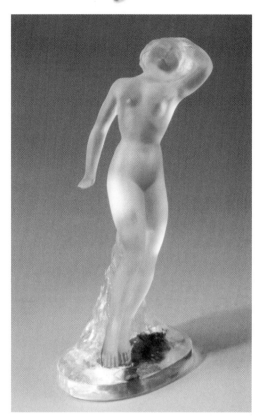

"Danseuse"

circa 1980, in clear and frosted glass, engraved Lalique France, 9 1/2" tall. (Lalique design No. 119080.)

$800-$900

"Grande Nue Socle Lierre"

a statuette, circa 1919, in clear and frosted glass with sepia patina, mounted on an ebony plinth, engraved R. Lalique, statuette 14" tall. (M p. 400, No. 836)

$16,000-$18,000

Figures

**"Perdrix Debout" and
"Perdrix Couchee"**
a pair of figures, circa 1939, in clear and frosted glass, stenciled R. LALIQUE and engraved R. Lalique, taller figure 7 1/4". (M p. 494, Nos. 1235 and 1236)

$500-$600/pair

"Groupe de Six Moineaux"
a decoration, in clear and frosted glass with gray patina, circa 1933, 11 5/8" long. (M p. 492, No. 1218)

$2,500+

"Moyenne Violee"
a statuette, circa 1912, in opalescent glass with blue patina, engraved Lalique, 5 3/8" tall. (M p. 398, No. 829)

$4,800-$5,300

"Moyenne Voilee"
a statuette, in clear and frosted glass with blue patina, engraved R. Lalique with original retailer's label. (Ref. M p. 398, No. 829)

$2,800-$3,100

"Source De La Fontaine Calypso"
a rare statuette, circa 1924, in clear and frosted glass, mounted on an ebonized wood plinth. Calypso is, together with three other models, the tallest in Lalique's range of 15 Source De La Fontaine statuettes, designed by Rene Lalique for use in a fountain that welcomed visitors to the Paris Exposition of 1925, wheel-cut R. LALIQUE, statuette 27" tall. (M p. 400, No. 837)

$22,000-$25,000

"Suzanne"

a statuette, in opalescent glass, with original bronze illuminating stand, molded R. LALIQUE, statuette 9 1/8" tall. (Ref. M p. 399, No. 833)

$25,000-$28,000

"Source De La Fountaine Clytie"

a rare statuette, circa 1924, in clear and frosted glass, mounted on an original wood base. Clytie is, together with three other models, the tallest in Lalique's range of 15 Source De La Fountaine statuettes, designed by Rene Lalique for use in a monumental fountain that welcomed visitors to the Paris Exposition of 1925, wheel-cut R. LALIQUE, 27" tall. (M p.401, No. 838)

$18,000-$20,000

"Suzanne"

a statuette, circa 1925, in opalescent glass with blue patina, molded R. LALIQUE, engraved R. Lalique France, statuette 9 1/8" tall. (M p. 399, No. 833)

$12,000-$15,000

"Suzanne"

a statuette, in amber glass, with original bronze illuminating stand, molded R. LALIQUE, statuette 9 1/8" tall. (M p. 399, No. 833)

$30,000+

Inkwells

"Biches"
in deep amber glass with white patina, circa 1912,
base 6" square. (M p. 315, No. 427)

$2,000+

"Cernay"
an inkwell, circa 1924, in clear glass with green
patina, molded R. LALIQUE, 15.5 cm. (M p. 318,
No. 437)

$1,400-$1,700

"Biches"
in black glass with white patina, circa 1912, base 6" square. (M p. 315, No. 427)

$2,000+

"Colbert"
in clear and frosted glass, circa 1924, 10 1/8" long. (M p. 318, No. 438)

$1,800+

"Mures"
in clear and frosted glass, circa 1920, 6" diameter. (M p. 316, No. 431)

$2,000+

"Escargots"
in clear and frosted glass, circa 1920, 6" diameter. (M p. 317, No. 433)

$2,500+

"Myrtilles"
in clear and frosted glass with black enamel decoration, circa 1924, 8 1/4" diameter. (M p. 318, No. 436)

$1,800+

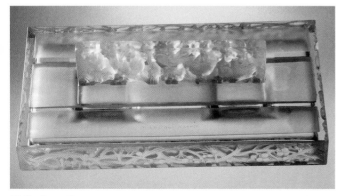

"Mirabeau"
in clear and frosted glass, circa 1927, 10 1/8" long. (M p. 319, No. 440)

$3,000+

"Nenuphar"
in satin glass, circa 1910, 3 1/3" diameter. (M p. 315, No. 425)

$1,200+

Inkwells

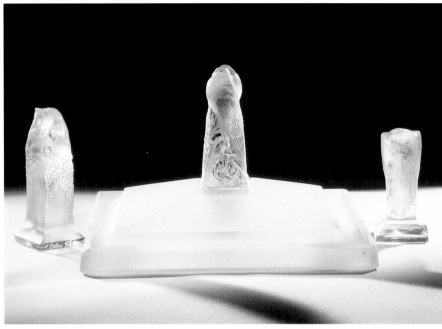

"Quatre Sirenes"
in clear and frosted glass with sepia patina, circa 1920, 6" diameter. (M p. 317, No. 434)

$3,500+

"Pigeons"
frosted glass base with clear and frosted stopper (same form as letter seal No. 186), shown with Aigle and Souris letters seals, circa 1912, base 8 5/8" square. (M p. 316, No. 430)

Inkwell only, $2,500+

"Quatre Sirenes"
in opalescent glass with sepia patina, circa 1920, 6" diameter. (M p. 317, No. 434)

$4,500+

"Serpents"
in clear and frosted glass, circa 1920, 6" diameter. (M p. 317, No. 432)

$3,000+

"Serpents"
in amber glass, circa 1920, 6" diameter. (M p. 317, No. 432)

$4,000+

"Sully"
in clear glass with black enamel, circa 1927, 9 7/8" long. (M p. 319, No. 439)

$4,000+

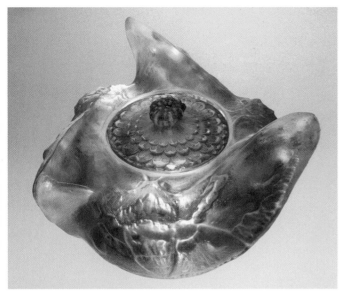

"Trois Papillons"
in opalescent glass with sepia patina, circa 1912, 3 7/8" diameter. (M p. 315, No. 426)

$2,000+

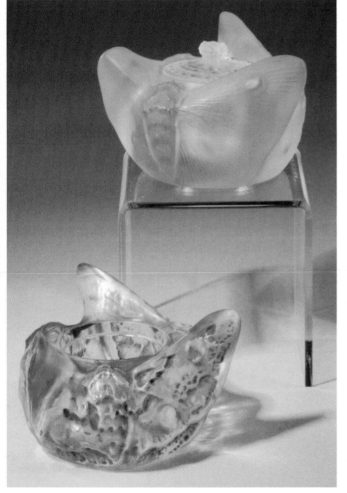

"Trois Papillons"
an inkwell and cover, circa 1912, in clear and frosted glass, engraved R. Lalique France, and molded R. LALIQUE, (later version with ridged wings), with an early version in clear and frosted glass with sepia patina, engraved Lalique, lacking cover, 3 1/2" diameter each. (M p. 315, No. 426)

$1,200-$1,400/pair

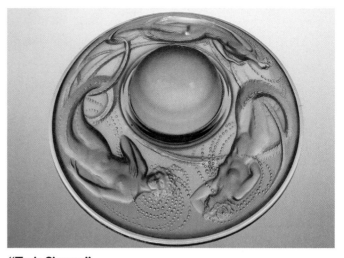

"Trois Sirenes"
in clear and frosted glass with sepia patina, circa 1921, 9 1/2" diameter. (M p. 317, No. 435)

$3,500+

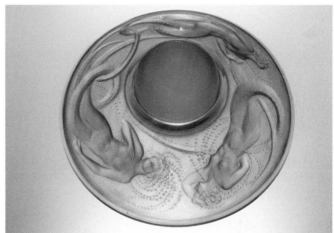

"Trois Sirenes"
in amber glass, circa 1921, 9 1/2" diameter. (M p. 317, No. 435)

$5,500+

"Trois Sirenes"
in opalescent glass, circa 1921, 9 1/2" diameter. (M p. 317, No. 435)

$4,000+

Jewelry

Jewelry design was Lalique's first love, and by the time he opened his shop in 1905, he had spent the better part of three decades perfecting his craft. As a result, Lalique jewelry often has a strong art nouveau influence. Glass production examples from the 1920s can still be purchased for less than $500. His original drawings of jewelry designs are also highly prized.

"Ange et Colombe"
a pendant, circa 1920, in clear and frosted glass with gilt backing and sepia patina, engraved R. Lalique, 1 3/4" diameter. (M p. 570, J)

$550-$650

"Barrette Oiseaux"
a glass and metal bar pin, circa 1912, the clear glass appearing violet from reflecting foil, brass backing stamped LALIQUE, 2 1/3" long. (M p. 541, No. 1351)

$550-$650

"Chose Promise"
a medallion for Fioret Fragrances, circa 1920, in clear and frosted glass, in silk-lined box. This example appears to be a prototype without the FIORET PARIS lettering, and unpierced for suspension, molded R. LALIQUE, 1 1/4" diameter. (M p. 937, No. 4)

$500-$600

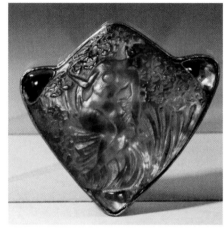

"Femmes dans les Fleurs"
a brooch, circa 1913, in blue glass and metal with gray patina, 2" long. (M p. 572, No. 1625)

$2,000-$2,500

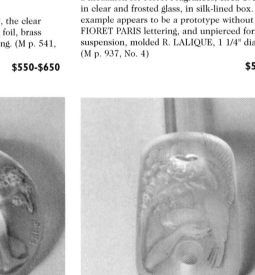

"Chose Promise"
a pendant for Fioret Perfume, in clear and frosted glass with gray patina, molded R. LALIQUE FIORET. (M p. 937, No. 4)

$300-$350

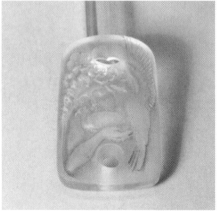

"Colombes"
a pendant, in pale opalescent glass with gray patina, engraved R. Lalique in script. (M p. 580, No. 1659)

$400-$500

"Feuilles"
a hatpin, circa 1912, in clear foil-backed glass, with sepia patina and original silvered metal mount, 9 3/4" long. (M p. 566, No. 1558)

$2,000-$2,200

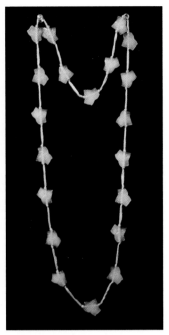

"Feuilles De Lierre"
a necklace with 20 elements, circa
1919, in opalescent green glass, on
original golden silk cord, engraved
R. Lalique, 40" long. (M p. 558, No.
1505)

$2,800-$3,200

"Gui"
a pendant, circa 1920, in yellow glass,
on modern beaded cord, molded
LALIQUE, 2" long. (M p. 579, No.
1655)

$400-$500

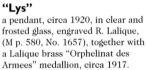

"Lys"
a pendant, circa 1920, in clear and
frosted glass, engraved R. Lalique,
(M p. 580, No. 1657), together with
a Lalique brass "Orphelinat des
Armees" medallion, circa 1917.

$500-$600/pair

"Meduse"
a green glass and gold ring, circa
1912, ring size 8, gold replaced. (M p.
527, No. 1253)

$500-$600

"Guepes"
a LALIQUE pendant, circa 1920, in
deep amber glass with sepia patina on
black silk cord, engraved Lalique, 2
1/8" tall. (M p. 578, No. 1650)

$700-$800

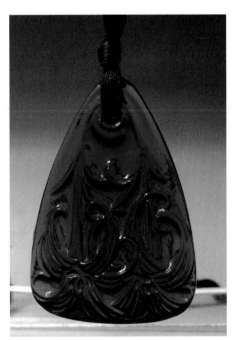

"Lys"
a pendant, in emerald green glass patterned with
pendant lilies, engraved R. Lalique in script, with
green silk hanging cord. (M p. 580, No. 1657)

$700-$800

"Muguet"
a lozenge-shaped pendant, circa 1921, in opalescent glass on
original green silk cord, molded R. LALIQUE, 1 3/4" long. (M p.
582, No. 1666)

$900-$1,000

Jewelry

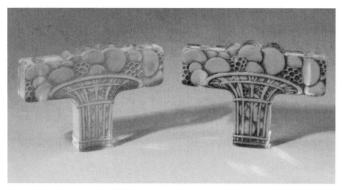

Two "Panier de Fruits" pendants
circa 1922, in clear and frosted glass, one with a sepia patina and one with a blue patina, engraved and stenciled marks, each 2" long. (M p. 583, No. 1670)

$600-$700/pair

"Panier de Fruits"
a pendant, circa 1922, in frosted glass with blue patina, engraved R. Lalique, 2" long. (M p. 583, No. 1670)

$300-$400

"Panier de Fruits"
a pendant, circa 1922, in frosted glass with sepia patina, engraved R. Lalique, 2" long. (M p. 583, No. 1670)

$300-$350

"Scarabees"
a metal hatpin, circa 1912, in clear and frosted glass with sepia patina, total length 9 7/8". (M p. 566, No. 1559)

$1,800-$2,000

"Scarabees"
a hatpin, circa 1912, in clear foil-backed glass, with sepia patina and original silvered metal mount, total length 9 3/4". (M p. 566, No. 1559)

$1,700-$2,000

"Trefles"
a pendant, in amber glass, patterned with cloverleaves, molded LALIQUE, 2 1/3" long. (M p. 580, No. 1656)

$1,000-$1,200

"Trefles"
a pendant, circa 1920, in yellow glass, molded LALIQUE, 2 1/3" long. (M p. 580, No. 1656)

$450-$550

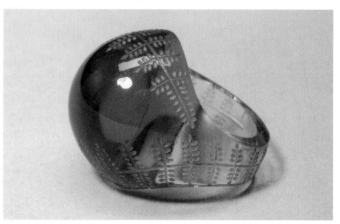

"Unie"
an engraved glass ring, circa 1931, in topaz glass, engraved with a stylized pattern of leaves, wheel-cut LALIQUE. This style of Lalique ring was produced blank and engraved with various designs, mostly representing foliage. (Ref. M p. 527, No. 1254)

$1,600-$1,800

An original design

for a necklace, circa 1900-05, pencil, ink, and watercolor on parchment paper, 8 5/8" by 11 1/8", together with a copy of the 1993 Paris Auction catalogue featuring the lot.

$1,800-$2,200

An original design

for a perfume bottle or veilleuse with "Marguerites" design, circa 1900-05, pencil, ink, and watercolor on parchment paper, 8 5/8" by 11 1/8", together with a copy of the 1993 Paris Auction catalogue featuring the lot.

$1,800-$2,200

An original design, "Chauntecler"

circa 1900-05, pencil, ink, and watercolor on parchment paper, 8 5/8" by 11 1/8", together with a copy of the 1993 Paris Auction catalogue featuring the lot.

$1,800-$2,200

"Pendentif Feuilles a Baies"

an original jewelry design drawn by Rene Lalique, circa 1898, ink and watercolor on parchment paper, depicting a swirl of leaves and berries, one berry with notation "diamant," paper size: 7 3/4" by 5 3/4".

$3,500-$4,000

"Pendentif Figurine a Glycine"

an original jewelry design drawn by Rene Lalique, circa 1898, ink and watercolor on parchment paper, depicting a draped female figure within a border of wisteria and jewels, numbered "8" upper left, 10 1/2" by 8 1/4".

$5,200-$5,500

Letter Seals

Despite their relatively small size, the intended use of letter seals and the damage common to these pieces can make perfect examples difficult to find, and prices have risen accordingly. Look for chips or cracks, especially on the undersides of the seals.

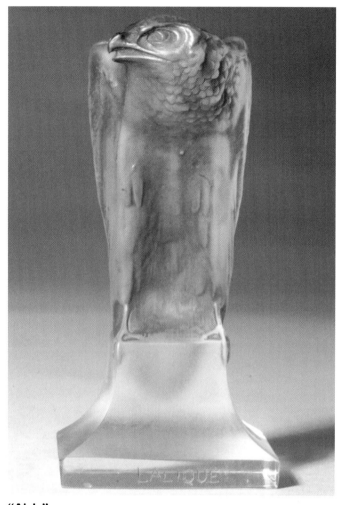

"Aigle"
in clear and frosted glass with charcoal gray patina, wheel-cut LALIQUE with original retailer's label, 3 1/2" tall. (Ref. M p. 249, No. 184)

$2,000-$2,500

"Aigle"
circa 1912, in clear and frosted glass with gray patina, engraved Lalique, 3 1/2" tall. (M p. 249, No. 184)

$1,700-$2,000

"Bressan"
in amber glass, circa 1931, 2 5/8" tall. (M p. 256, No. 232)

$1,500+

"Cigognes"
circa 1919, in clear and frosted glass with gray patina, molded LALIQUE, 2 3/4" tall. (M p. 253, No. 213)

$800-$1,000

"Figurine"
in clear and frosted glass, circa 1919, 2 3/4" tall. (M p. 252, No. 203)

$1,200+

"Hirondelles"
circa 1919, in clear and frosted glass with gray patina, engraved R. Lalique, 2 1/8" tall. (M p. 250, No. 188)

$1,400+

"Gros Bourdon"
a letter seal or door handle, circa 1910, in clear and frosted glass with charcoal patina, engraved R. Lalique, 2 1/3" tall. (M p. 253, No. 208)

$2,800-$3,400

"Hirondelles"
in clear and frosted glass, circa 1919, 2 1/8" tall. (M p. 250, No. 188)

$1,000+

"Lapin"
circa 1925, in topaz glass, engraved R. Lalique France, 2 1/4" tall. (M p. 254, No. 214)

$500-$600

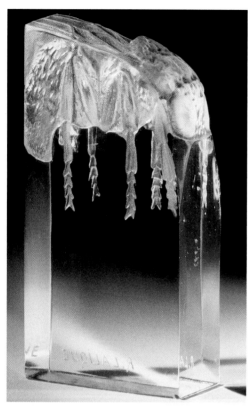

"Mouche"
in clear and frosted glass, circa 1912, 2 1/2" tall. (M p. 249, No. 180)

$1,200+

"Perruche"
in clear and frosted glass, circa 1919. (M p. 247, D)

$900+

"Perruches"
in clear and frosted glass, circa 1919, 2 1/8" tall. (M p. 250, No. 187)

$900+

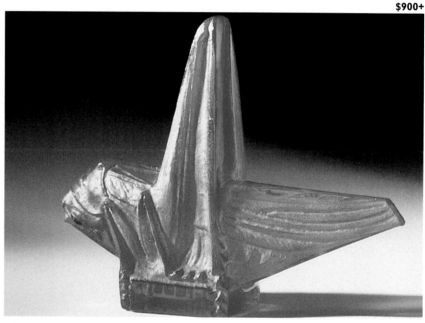

"Sauterelles"
circa 1912, in electric blue glass, molded LALIQUE, 1 5/8" tall. (M p. 249, No. 183)

$1,000-$1,200

"Pigeons"
in clear and frosted glass, circa 1912, 4" tall. (M p. 249, No. 186)

$1,500+

"Souris"
in opalescent mint green glass, engraved R. Lalique France. (Ref. M p. 254, No. 218)

$600-$700

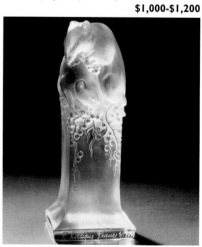

"Souris"
in clear and frosted glass, circa 1912, 4 1/8" tall. (M p. 249, No. 185)

$700+

"Statuette Drapee"
circa 1912, in clear and frosted glass with green patina, engraved Lalique, 2 1/2" tall. (M p. 249, No. 181)

$2,900-$3,300

"Tete D'Aigle"
circa 1911, in black glass with whitish patina, engraved Lalique, 3 1/8" tall. (M p. 248, No. 175)

$1,400-$1,600

"Tete D'Aigle"
circa 1911, in clear and frosted glass with sepia patina, engraved Lalique, 3 1/8" tall. (M p. 248, No. 175)

$1,200-$1,400

"Trois Papillons"
in clear and frosted glass, circa 1919, 2 5/8" tall. (M p. 251, No. 197)

$900+

"Statuette Drapee"
in blue glass with white patina, circa 1912, 2 1/2" tall. (M p. 249, No. 181)

$5,500+

"Tete D'Aigle"
circa 1911, in clear and frosted glass with gray patina, engraved Lalique and with intaglio monogram CH, possibly for Charles Haviland, 3 1/8" tall. (M p. 248, No. 175)

$1,400-$1,600

"Victoire"
circa 1920, in clear and frosted glass with sepia patina, molded LALIQUE, engraved with intaglio monogram, 1 3/4" tall. (M p. 253, No. 210)

$1,000-$1,300

Lighting

Lalique lighting fixtures have always been a rarity, and pieces priced in the low five figures are not uncommon. Look for examples with original hardware, stands, cords, and wiring.

"Coquilles"
a pair of wall sconces, in opalescent glass, of demi-lune design with metal fittings and electrified, wheel-cut LALIQUE FRANCE. (Ref. M p. 677, No. 2008)

$2,800-$3,200

"Dahlias"
a ceiling light, in clear and frosted glass with sepia patina, molded R. LALIQUE. (Ref. M p. 671, No. 2459)

$2,800-$3,200

"Bague Feuilles"
a table lamp, circa 1912, in clear and frosted glass with sepia patina, wheel-cut R. LALIQUE, 17 1/2" tall. (M p. 617, No. 2150)

$18,000-$20,000

"Fauvettes A"
an illuminating surtout de table, circa 1930, in clear and frosted glass with original nickel-plated metal illuminating base, wheel-cut R. LALIQUE, 13 1/2" tall. (M p. 486, No. 1171)

$11,000-$13,000

"Gros Poisson Algues"
a model of a large fish on illuminating stand, in clear, polished glass, the bronze stand fitted with illuminating system including red glass light filter, wheel-cut R. LALIQUE FRANCE to glass, base molded R. LALIQUE, glass with large crack in base. (M p. 478, No. 1100)
$2,500-$3,000

"Monaco"
a hanging chandelier, designed by Marc Lalique, circa 1950, in clear, polished glass, formed as eight tentacle-like arms issuing from a metal cage with star-form finial, includes original ceiling cap, lacks hanging rod and one glass finial, engraved Lalique, 32" diameter.
$2,800-$3,200

A "Laussane" corner sconce
in clear and frosted glass. (M p. 677, No. 2040)
$300-$350

"Lierre"
a ceiling light, circa 1927, in clear and frosted glass with sepia patina, with original hooks and hanging cord, molded R. FRANCE, 14 1/2" diameter. (M p. 674, No. 2469)
$3,500-$4,000

"Six Danseuses"
a table lamp, circa 1931, in clear and frosted glass with sepia patina, molded R. LALIQUE, 10" tall. (M p. 625, No. 2179)
$15,000-$17,000

Metalware

Bronze medallion
issued to mark the opening of Lalique's gallery in Paris, 1905, 2 1/2" diameter.

No established value

"Les Parfums De Coty"
a rare gilt metal plaque for Coty, circa 1911, signed in the mold R. Lalique, 3" by 2". Plaques of this type were attached to the interior of tester boxes. (M p. 928, No. 2)

$600-$700

"Les Parfums De Coty"
a rare gilt metal plaque for Coty, circa 1911, signed in the mold R. Lalique, 3" by 1/2". Plaques of this type were attached to the interior of tester boxes. (M p. 928, No. 2)

$600-$700

"Parfums Fontanis"
a rare gilt metal plaque for Fontanis, circa 1925, signed in the mold R. Lalique, approximately 3" by 2 1/2". Plaques of this type were attached to the interior of tester boxes. (M p. 937, No. 2)

$1,200+

"Anemones"
a large round mirror, circa 1913. (M p. 356, C)

$2,500+

Mirrors

"Deux Figurines"
a hand mirror, in silver with original case, circa 1912, 13 7/8" long. (M p. 359, No. 676)

$2,000+

"Entrelacs"
a wall mirror, in clear glass with gilded highlights, on nickel-plated metal frame, the design circa 1934, this example circa 1951, 33" by 25 1/2", complete with assembly hardware and components. This is the large version of Entrelacs, which was produced in limited number with gilded highlights until the early 1950s. (M p. 259, G)

$18,000-$22,000

"Deux Oiseaux"
a round hand mirror, circa 1914, 6 1/3" diameter. (M p. 359, No. 677)

$900+

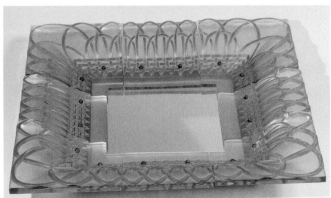

"Entrelacs"
a mirror or picture frame, in clear glass with gilded highlights, circa 1934. (M p. 259, G)

$8,000-$10,000

Mirrors

"Festons"
a mirror frame, in clear and frosted glass, circa 1932, 15" tall. (M p. 265, No. 265)

$10,000+

"Fronton Panier de Fleur"
a wall mirror, circa 1933, in clear and frosted glass, with original metal back and mirror plate, stenciled R. LALIQUE FRANCE, 55" by 20". (M p. 363, No. 689)

$22,000-$26,000

"Muguet"
a hand mirror, circa 1921, in clear and frosted glass and metal, with silk tassel, molded R. LALIQUE, 6 1/3" diameter. (M p. 361, No.684)

$700-$800

"Perles"
a mirror frame, in clear and frosted glass, circa 1926. (M p. 258, B)

$5,000+

"Tete"
an oval mirror back, in clear and frosted glass, patterned with female head, lacks mirror and metal frame. (M p. 361, No. 682)

$500-$600

Panels

"Hirondelles"
light panel in clear and frosted glass, 1928, 17 3/4" tall. (M p. 591, No. 2006)

$10,000+

Glass ceiling panel
from the Coty boutique in New York, 1912, clear and frosted glass with sepia patina.

$15,000

Glass column panel
sections from the Coty boutique in New York, 1912, clear and frosted glass with sepia patina.

$15,000+ each

Panels

"Jeune Faune"
a pair of architectural panels, circa 1929, in clear and frosted glass,
each 12" by 4". (M p. 879, No. 4)

$6,500-$7,000/pair

"Oiseaux et Spirales"
section of a wall panel in clear and frosted glass, 1929, 11 7/8" by 5 3/4". (M p. 880, No. 5)

$30,000+/pair

"Merles et Raisins"
panel in clear and frosted glass with sepia patina, 1928, in steel frame, panel
20" tall. (M p. 865)

$20,000+

Window panel
from Chapelle de la
Vierge Fidele a la
Deliverande, Calvados,
Normandy, France,
1930.

$20,000+

Paperweights

The Lalique factory still produces seven paperweights today, which were originally made as car mascots: Chrysis, eagle's head, small cock, boar, perch, St. Christopher, and the cock's head. Some contemporary weights—made as recently as the 1970s—may be valued at less that $100 each, while the vintage pieces in colored glass can top $2,000.

"Antilope"
circa 1929, in clear and frosted glass, engraved R. Lalique France, 3 1/3" tall. (M p. 384, No. 1148)

$650-$750

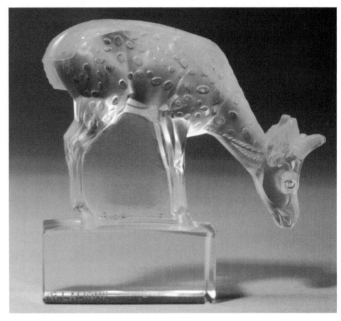

"Daim"
in clear and frosted glass, molded and stenciled R. LALIQUE, 3 1/3" tall. (Ref. M p. 389, No. 1168)

$900-$1,200

"Deux Aigles"
circa 1914, in deep amber glass, wheel-cut R. Lalique, 3" tall. (M p. 380, No. 801)

$600-$700

"Deux Tourterelles"
in gray-blue glass, circa 1925, 4 3/4" tall. (M p. 381, No. 1128)

$2,500+

"Deux Tourterelles"
circa 1925, in topaz glass, stenciled R. LALIQUE FRANCE, 4 3/4" tall. (M p. 381, No. 1128)

$2,200-$2,600

Paperweights

"Moineau Hardi"
circa 1929, in clear and frosted glass, engraved R. LALIQUE, 3 1/2" tall. (M p. 385, No. 1150)

$350-$400

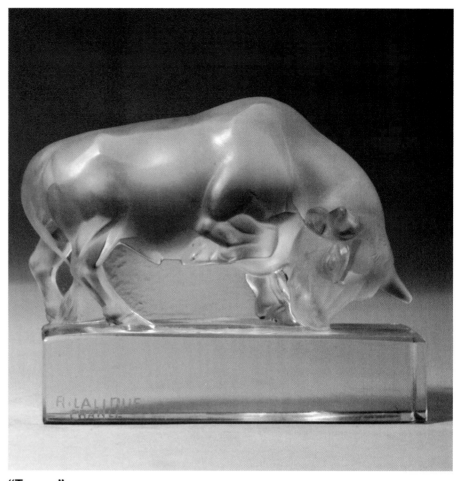

"Moineau Moqueur"
circa 1930, in clear and frosted glass, stenciled R. LALIQUE, 3 1/3" tall. (M p. 389, No. 1167)

$350-$400

"Taureau"
in clear and frosted glass, wheel-cut R. LALIQUE FRANCE. (M p. 391, No. 1194)

$900-$1,200

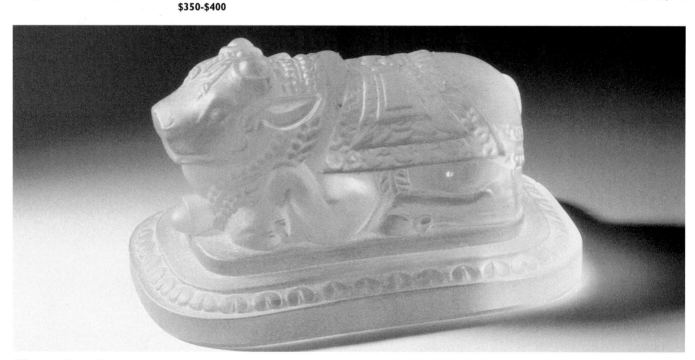

"Taureau Sacre"
in clear and frosted glass, circa 1938, 1/2" tall. (M p. 379, C)

$1,800+

"Toby"
circa 1931, in clear and frosted glass, stenciled R. LALIQUE FRANCE, 3 1/3" tall. (M p. 391, No. 1192)

$1,700-$2,000

Three animal-form paperweights
circa 1975, comprising "Daim," "Bison," and "Tang Horse," all engraved Lalique France.

$250-$300/set

Three modern bird paperweights
circa 1970, comprising a pair of "Moineau Moqueur" and "Moineau Hardi," all engraved Lalique France, average 3 1/2" tall.

$175-$225/set

Perfume Containers

Lalique opened his first Paris retail shop in 1905, near the perfume business of François Coty. Coty commissioned Lalique to design his perfume labels in 1907, and Lalique also created his first perfume bottles for Coty. There are more than 250 different bottles known, with prices ranging from less than $200 to several thousand dollars. Those with elaborate and figural stoppers command a premium. This section features perfume atomizers, bottles, and burners.

Atomizers

"4 Figurines"
two perfume atomizers for Marcas et Bardel, circa 1927, in clear and frosted glass with chrome fittings, both molded R. LALIQUE MADE IN FRANCE, taller 6 1/2". (M p. 962, No. 6)
$850-$950/pair

"Epines"
a perfume atomizer with metal mount, circa 1920, in clear and frosted glass with blue patina, together with "Elizabeth," a modern perfume bottle. Epines molded R. LALIQUE FRANCE, 4 1/8" tall. (M p. 351, No. 653)
$550-$650/pair

"Epines"
a perfume atomizer with metal mount, circa 1920, in clear and frosted glass, stenciled R. LALIQUE FRANCE, overall height 4 1/8". (M p. 351, No. 653)
$175-$225

"Calendal"
a perfume atomizer for Molinard, in clear and frosted glass, with original box, circa 1927, 5 1/2" tall. (M p. 963, Molinard 2/A)
$600+

"Figurines"
a perfume atomizer for Marcas et Bardel, in clear and frosted glass, with original tasseled bulb, circa 1924, 3 3/4" tall. (M p. 961, Marcas et Bardel 1/B)
$350+

"Figurines et Guirlandes"
three perfume atomizers for Molinard, 1920s, in clear and frosted glass with brass fittings, all molded R. LALIQUE MADE IN FRANCE, tallest 4 1/2". (M p. 963)

$1,000-$1,300/set

Two perfume atomizers
circa 1920, in clear glass with green patina and brass fittings, comprising "Muguet" for Macy's and "Semis du Fleurs" for Sussfeld, both molded R. LALIQUE MADE IN FRANCE, each 4 1/4" tall. (M pp. 961 and 963)

$900-$1,100/pair

Three perfume atomizers
1920s, in clear and frosted glass with brass fittings, two with blue patina, comprising "Le Parisienne" for Molinard, "Muguet" for Macy's, and "Semis du Fleurs" for Sussfeld, All molded R. LALIQUE, tallest 6". (M p. 963, No. 1A and p. 961, No. 1A)

$900-$1,000/set

"Origan"
two perfume atomizers, 1924, for D'Heraud, in clear glass with charcoal patina and brass fittings, both molded R. LALIQUE, 7" tall. (M p. 961, No. 1)

$800-$900/pair

Two perfume atomizers
in clear and frosted glass, comprising "Fleurettes," with sepia patina, and "Figurines et Guirlandes" for Molinard, both with molded signatures, 6" and 4" tall. (M pp. 351 and 963)

$350-$400/pair

Five perfume atomizers
circa 1920-1960, comprising "Calendal," circa 1923, for Worth in clear and frosted glass with green patina, together with two for Worth and two for Nina Ricci, 5" tall. (M p. 963, No. 2B)

$900-$1,000/set

Perfume Containers
Display perfume bottles

"Dans La Nuit"
a display perfume bottle for Worth, circa 1924, in clear and frosted glass with blue enamel, molded R. LALIQUE, engraved Lalique France, 9 1/2" tall. (M p. 952, No. 4)

$1,200-$1,400

"Je Reviens"
a display perfume bottle for Worth, circa 1932, in dark and light blue glass, molded LALIQUE MADE IN FRANCE, 11 1/4" tall. (M p. 953, B)

$600-$700

"L'Air Du Temps"
a display perfume bottle for Nina Ricci, circa 1960, in clear and frosted glass, sealed and with contents, 12 1/2" tall.

$900-$1,000

Perfume bottles

"A Coeur Joie"
a perfume bottle for Nina Ricci, in clear and frosted glass, with original box, circa 1942, in three sizes ranging from 3 1/2" to 6" tall. (M p. 946)

$400-$700

"Ambre"
a perfume bottle for D'Orsay, circa 1912, in black glass with white patina, molded LALIQUE, 5 1/8" tall. (M p. 933, D'Orsay 4)

$2,200-$2,600

"Ambre"
a perfume bottle for D'Orsay, circa 1912, in black glass, molded LALIQUE, 5 1/8" tall. (M p. 933, No. 1)

$1,300-$1,500

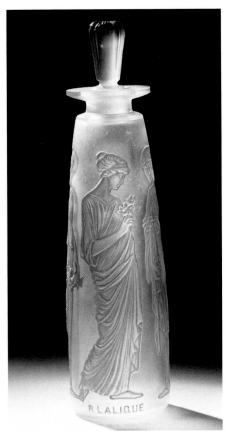

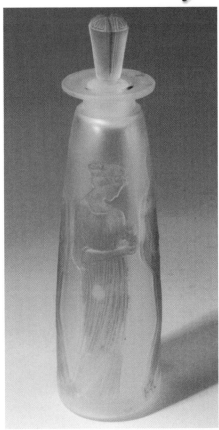

"Ambre Antique"
a perfume bottle for Coty, in clear and frosted glass with sepia patina, sharp mold and strong color, molded LALIQUE, 6 1/4" tall with stopper. (M p. 927, Coty 3)

$3,500-$4,000

"Ambre Antique"
a perfume bottle for Coty, circa 1910, in clear and frosted glass with sepia patina, molded R. LALIQUE, 6" tall. (M p. 927, No. 3)

$1,600-$1,800

"L'Ambre De Vigny"
a perfume bottle for De Vigny, in clear and frosted glass, circa 1925, 6" tall. (M p. 930, De Vigny 3)

$1,500+

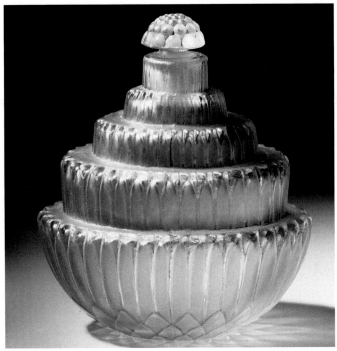

"Ambroise"
in clear and frosted glass, circa 1928, 3" tall. (M p. 337, No. 523)

$1,200+

"Amelie"
a perfume bottle, circa 1927, in clear and frosted glass, engraved R. LALIQUE FRANCE No. 520, 2 7/8" tall. (M p. 336, No. 520)

$800-$1,000

Perfume Containers

"Amphitrite"
a perfume bottle, circa 1920, in clear and frosted glass with strong blue patina, molded R. LALIQUE, engraved France, No. 514, 3 3/4" tall. (M p. 335, No. 514)
$2,700-$3,000

"Amphitrite"
in iridescent green glass, circa 1920, 3 3/4" tall. (M p. 335, No. 514)
$4,000-$5,000

"Amphitrite"
a perfume bottle, circa 1920, in clear and frosted glass with traces of blue patina, engraved R. Lalique France, No. 514, 3 3/4" tall. (M p. 335, No. 514)
$1,800-$2,000

"Au Coeur des Calices"
a perfume bottle for Coty, in blue glass, molded LALIQUE, stopper frozen. (Ref. M p. 929, No. 20)
$3,500-$4,000

"Bouchon Mures"
bottle in clear glass with enamel decoration, stopper in amber glass, circa 1920, 4 1/3" tall. (M p. 329, No. 495)

$3,000+

"Bouquet De Faunes"
a perfume bottle for Guerlain, circa 1925, in clear and frosted glass, 4" tall. (M p. 940, No. 1)

$800-$900

"Cactus"
Three modern items, comprising a perfume bottle and powder box in the "Cactus" pattern with black enamel details, and "Chloe," a box with gilt metal mounts, all engraved Lalique France. Bottle 4 3/4" tall.

$350-$450/set

"Cactus"
Three perfume bottles, 1930s, comprising a "Cactus," stenciled R. LALIQUE FRANCE and with ROYAL DUTCH MAIL, and two "Roses Sans Fin" bottles for ARYS, molded R. LALIQUE ARYS, tallest 3 7/8". (M p. 336, Nos. 519, 923 and 5)

$600-$700/set

Perfume Containers

"Camille"
a perfume bottle, circa 1927, in clear and frosted glass, molded R. LALIQUE FRANCE, 2 1/4" tall. (M p. 335, No. 516)

$600-$700

"Camille"
in green glass with white patina, circa 1927, 2 1/3" tall. (M p. 335, No. 516)

$1,500+

"Chypre"
a perfume bottle for Houbigant, in clear and frosted glass, circa 1925, 3 1/8" tall. (M p. 941, Houbigant 4)

$500+

"Chypre"
a perfume bottle for Forvil, in clear and frosted glass, circa 1924, in two sizes, 3" and 3 1/2" tall. (M p. 938, Forvil 6)

$900+

"Cigalia"
a perfume bottle for Roger et Gallet, in clear and frosted glass, circa 1925, 7 1/4" tall. (M p. 948, Roger et Gallet 11)

$1,200+

"Clairefontaine"
in clear and frosted glass, circa 1931, 4 3/4" tall. (M p. 338, No. 526)

$1,800+

"Clairfontaine"
a pair of perfume bottles, designed in 1931, these examples 1950-1980, in clear and frosted glass, various mvarks, 5" tall.

$500-$600/pair

"Clamart"
in smoky satin glass with black patina, circa 1927, 4 1/2" tall. (M p. 336, No. 517)

$1,800+

"Coeur Joie"
a perfume bottle for Nina Ricci, circa 1955, in clear and frosted glass, engraved Lalique France, 6" tall.

$400-$500

"Colgate"
a perfume bottle for Colgate, in clear and frosted glass with black enamel detailing, molded R. LALIQUE MADE IN FRANCE. (M p. 926, No. 1)

$900-$1,000

"Colgate"
a perfume bottle in clear glass with black enamel, for Colgate, circa 1925, molded R. LALIQUE, 3 1/3" tall. (M p. 926, No. 1)

$1,100-$1,400

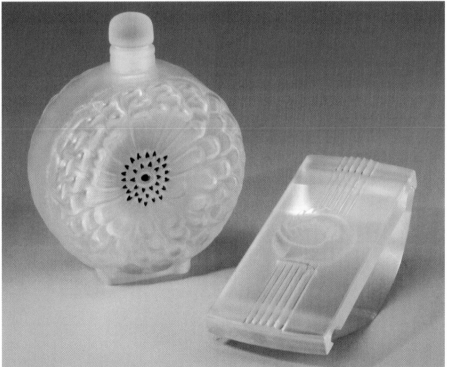

"Dahlia"
Two modern items: a "Dahlia" pattern perfume bottle, in clear glass with black enamel highlights, 7" tall, together with a clear glass and brass rocker blotter, patterned with an exotic bird, 7" long.

$300-$400/pair

"Danae"
a perfume bottle for Louvre (Magasin Du), in clear and frosted glass, circa 1930, 3 1/8" tall. (M p. 944, Louvre (Magasin Du) 1)

$3,000+

"Dans la Nuit"
a perfume bottle for Worth, in blue glass, circa 1924, 2 1/3" tall. (M p. 951, Worth 2)

$1,800+

"Danseuse et Phalenes"
a perfume bottle for Erasmic, in clear glass with sepia patina, circa 1925, 3 1/3" tall. (M p. 936, Erasmic)

$3,500+

"Dans la Nuit"
a perfume bottle for Worth, in clear and frosted glass with cobalt blue patina, circa 1924, in sizes ranging from 3 1/8" to 9 7/8" tall. (M p. 951, Worth 1)

$1,800-$2,500

"Deux Anemones"
a modern perfume bottle, and "Anemones," an ornament, both in clear and frosted glass with black enamel, both Engraved Lalique France, perfume 6 1/3" tall.
$250-$300/pair

"Enfants" and "Deux Fleurs,"
two modern perfume bottles, both engraved Lalique France, taller 3 3/4".
$250-$325/pair

"Eau de Toilette"
a perfume bottle for Coty, in clear and frosted glass, circa 1911, in sizes ranging from 3 1/8" to 7 7/8" tall. (M p. 928, Coty 11)
$400-$800

"Deux Figurines, Bouchon Figurines"
in clear and frosted glass, circa 1912, 4 3/4" tall. (M p. 328, No. 490)
$1,200+

"Entrelacs"
a perfume bottle for Volnay, in clear and frosted glass with sepia patina, circa 1925, 3 1/3" tall. (M p. 951, Volnay 12)
$700+

"En Croisiere"
a perfume bottle for Worth, in clear and frosted glass, with original box, circa 1935, in sizes ranging from 1 3/4" to 3 1/8" tall. (M p. 954, Worth 21)
$600+

"Epines No. 4"
a perfume bottle, circa 1920, in clear and frosted glass with gray patina, engraved R. Lalique France, 3 1/4" tall. (M p. 343, No. 593)
$450-$550

Perfume Containers

"Feuilles Stylisees"
a perfume bottle for Arys, in satin glass, circa 1920, 5" tall. (M p. 924, Arys 13)

$700+

"Flausa"
a perfume bottle for Roger et Gallet, in clear and frosted glass with sepia patina, circa 1914, 4 3/4" tall. (M p. 947, Roger et Gallet 3)

$1,800+

"Fille d'Eve"
a perfume bottle for Nina Ricci, in clear and frosted glass, with original paper label and silk lined presentation box in the form of a wicker basket with bow, engraved Lalique France Nina Ricci.

$550-$650

"Fleurettes"
a perfume bottle, circa 1919, in clear and frosted glass with blue patina, molded LALIQUE with extended L, 6 1/3" tall. (M p. 341, No. 576)

$500-$600

"Fleurs Concave"
a perfume bottle, circa 1912, in clear and frosted glass with blue patina, engraved R. Lalique France, 4 1/4" tall. (M p. 327, No. 486)

$1,200-$1,400

"Fougeres"
in green glass, circa 1912, 3 1/2" tall. (M p. 328, No. 489)

$3,000+

"Fox Trot"
a perfume bottle for Arys, in clear and frosted glass, circa 1919, 5 1/2" tall. (M p. 923, Arys 4)

$1,200+

"Floride"
a perfume bottle and goblet, circa 1965, in clear and teal glass, engraved Lalique France, perfume 6" tall.

$450-$550/pair

"Frise Fleurs"
a perfume bottle for Raquel Meller, in clear and frosted glass with enamel decoration, circa 1925, 3" tall. (M p. 947)

$2,500+

Perfume Containers

"Glycines"
a perfume bottle for Gabilla, clear and frosted glass with blue-gray patina, circa 1925, 4 1/8" tall. (M p. 940, Gabilla 3)

$1,400-$1,600

"Gregoire"
in clear and frosted glass, circa 1927, 3 7/8" tall. (M p. 337, No. 521)

$900+

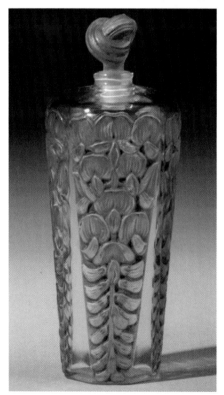

"Glycines"
a perfume bottle for Gabilla, circa 1925, in clear and frosted glass with blue patina, molded R. LALIQUE PARIS FRANCE, 4 1/8" tall. (M p. 940, No. 3)

$1,400-$1,600

"Helene"
(Lotus), a perfume bottle, circa 1928, in clear and frosted glass, stenciled R. LALIQUE FRANCE, 2 5/8" tall. (M p. 337, No. 522)

$1,800-$2,100

"Hirondelles"
in clear and frosted glass with gray patina, circa 1920, 3 1/2" tall. (M p. 332, No. 503)

$1,800+

"Jardinee"
a perfume bottle for Volnay, in clear and frosted glass with sepia patina, circa 1922, 5" tall. (M p. 950, Volnay 8)

$1,500+

"Je Reviens"
a lotion bottle for Worth, in cobalt blue glass, circa 1931, 4" tall. (M p. 953, Worth 16)

$2,000+

"Imperial"
a perfume bottle for Khouri (Lenghyal), in clear and frosted glass, circa 1936, in two sizes, 2 1/2" and 3 1/3" tall. (M p. 943)

$1,200+

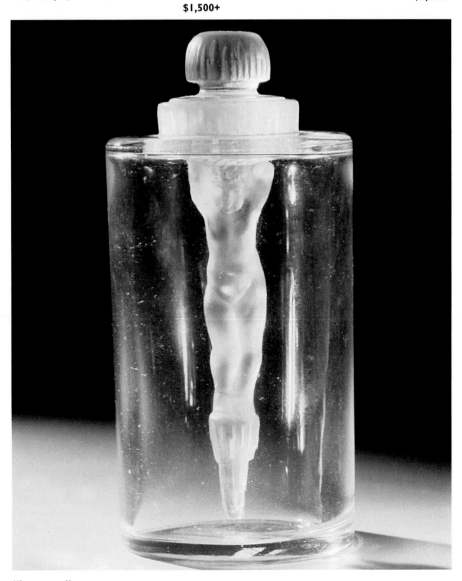

"Imprudence"
a perfume bottle for Worth, in clear glass with black enamel decoration (worn), circa 1938; in sizes ranging from 2 1/3" to 8 7/8" tall. (M p. 954, Worth 24)

$1,400-$1,800

"Jeunesse"
in clear and frosted glass, circa 1933, 4 1/8" tall. (M p. 338, No. 528)

$4,000+

Perfume Containers

"La Belle Saison"
a perfume bottle for Houbigant, circa 1925, in clear and frosted glass with sepia patina, molded R. LALIQUE MADE IN FRANCE, 4 1/2" tall. (M p. 941, No. 3)
$1,100-$1,300

"La Violette"
a perfume bottle for Gabilla, circa 1925, in clear glass with violet enamel, molded LALIQUE, 3 1/3" tall. (M p. 940, No. 2)
$3,000-$3,500

"La Belle Saison"
a perfume bottle for Houbigant, in clear and frosted glass with strong brown patina, and original box, circa 1925, in two sizes, 4" and 5 1/2" tall. (M p. 941, Houbigant 3)
$2,000-$2,500

"Le Jade"
a perfume bottle for Roger et Gallet, in opalescent green glass, circa 1926, molded R. LALIQUE, 3 1/8" tall. (M p. 948, Roger et Gallet 15)
$2,700-$3,200

"Lentilles"
in clear and frosted glass with black enamel decoration, circa 1912, 2" tall. (M p. 327, No. 485)

$2,200

"Le Parfum Des Anges"
a perfume bottle for Oviatt of Los Angeles, circa 1928, in clear and frosted glass with sepia patina, molded R. LALIQUE FRANCE, 3 1/4" tall. (M p. 946, No.1)

$1,800-$2,000

"Les Cinq Fleurs"
a perfume bottle for Forvil, in clear and frosted glass with black enamel decoration, and original box, circa 1926, in sizes ranging from 2 1/2" to 9 7/8" tall. (M p. 938, Forvil 13)

$1,500

"Le Lys"
a perfume bottle for D'Orsay, in clear glass with sepia patina, circa 1922, in sizes ranging from 3 1/8" to 9 7/8" tall. (M p. 935, D'Orsay 19)

$1,200

"Le Jade"
a jade green glass perfume bottle for Roger et Gallet, circa 1926, molded R. LALIQUE, 3 1/8" tall. (M p. 948, No. 15)

$2,700-$3,200

Perfume Containers

"Lilas"
a perfume bottle for Gabilla, in clear and frosted glass, circa 1925, 3 1/2" tall. (M p. 940, Gabilla 1)

$1,200

"Le Succes"
a perfume bottle for D'Orsay, in satin glass, circa 1914, 3 3/4" tall. (M p. 934, D'Orsay 7)

$1,800

"Lilas"
a perfume bottle for Gabilla, in clear and frosted glass with strong sepia patina, circa 1925, 3 1/2" tall. (M p. 940, Gabilla 1)

$1,400

"Lunaria"
in clear and frosted glass with sepia patina, circa 1912, 3 1/8" tall. (M p. 326, No. 482)

$1,500+

"Les Yeux Bleus"
a perfume bottle for Canarina, in blue glass with original box, circa 1928, 2" tall. (M p. 925, Canarina 1)

$2,000+

"Marquila"
in satin glass, circa 1927, 3 1/3" tall. (M p. 335, No. 515)

$900+

"Mimeomai"
a perfume bottle for Volnay, in clear and frosted glass, circa 1922, 4 3/4" tall. (M p. 950, Volnay 5)

$1,400+

"Misti"
a perfume bottle for Piver (L.T.), in clear and frosted glass, circa 1920, 2 1/8" tall. (M p. 946, Piver (L.T.) 1)

$1,500+

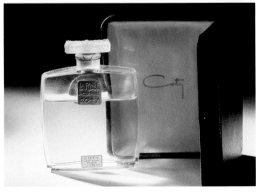

"Muguet"
a perfume bottle for Coty, in clear and frosted glass, with original box, circa 1912, in two sizes, 3 1/8" and 4" tall. (M p. 929, Coty 21) (Baccarat also made a Muguet bottle for Coty.)

$400+

"Muguet"
in clear and frosted glass, circa 1931, 4" tall. (M p. 338, No. 525)

$1,500+

"Muguet"
a perfume bottle, circa 1931, in clear and frosted glass with green patina, stenciled R. LALIQUE FRANCE, 4" tall. (M p. 338, No. 525)

$1,900-$2,300

Perfume Containers

"Mystere"
a perfume bottle for D'Orsay, circa 1912, in black glass with white patina, molded LALIQUE, 3 3/4" tall. (M p. 933, No. 2)

$850-$1,000

"Niobe"
a perfume bottle for Violet, in clear and frosted glass with sepia patina, circa 1919, 4 1/8" tall. (M p. 949)

$900+

"Oree"
a perfume bottle for Claire, circa 1930, in clear and frosted glass with sepia patina. Stopper molded LALIQUE, base molded FRANCE, with paper label from the Wanamaker Stores, 3 1/8" tall. (M p. 996, No. 1)

$2,600-$2,800

"Palerme"
a perfume bottle, circa 1926, in clear glass, molded
R. LALIQUE, 4 1/2" tall. (M p. 336, No. 518)
$600-$700

"Paquerettes"
a perfume bottle for Roger et Gallet, in clear and frosted glass with patina, circa 1919, 3 1/8" tall. (M p. 947, Roger et Gallet 5)
$4,000-$4,500

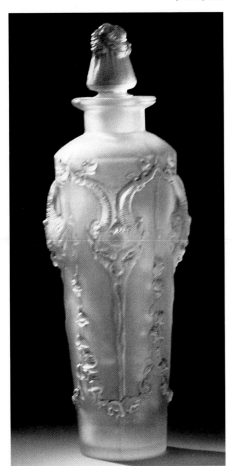

"Pan"
a perfume bottle, circa 1920, in clear and frosted glass with gray patina, molded R. LALIQUE, 5" tall. (M p. 332, No. 504)
$1,200-$1,400

"Paquerettes"
a perfume bottle for Roger et Gallet, in clear and frosted glass with sepia patina, molded LALIQUE. (M p. 947, No. 5)
$4,000-$4,500

"Parfums"
a perfume bottle for Forvil, in clear and frosted glass with sepia patina, circa 1922; in sizes ranging from 3 1/8" to 4 3/4" tall. (M p. 938, Forvil 9)
$900+

Perfume Containers

"Penier De Roses"
a perfume bottle, circa 1912, in clear and frosted glass with sepia patina, molded LALIQUE, 4" tall. (M p. 327, No. 487)

$3,000-$3,500

"Perles"
a perfume bottle, circa 1926, in opalescent glass, molded R. LALIQUE, 5 1/3" tall. (M p. 344, No. 602)

$600-$700

"Perles"
a perfume bottle, in opalescent glass with sepia patina, molded R. LALIQUE, 5 1/2" tall. (M p. 344, No. 601)

$1,500-$1,800

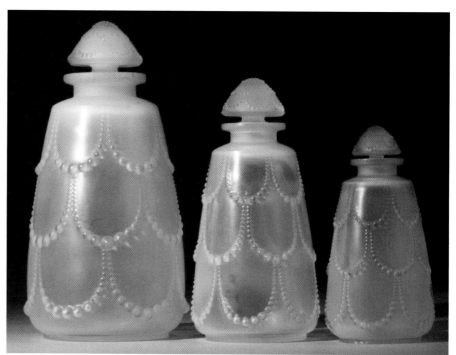

"Petites Fleurs"
in clear and frosted glass with sepia patina, circa 1910, 4" tall. (M p. 325, No. 478)

$900+

"Perles"
a garniture of three perfume bottles, circa 1926, in opalescent glass, molded or stenciled R. LALIQUE, tallest 8 1/8". (M p. 344, Nos. 600, 601, and 602)

$2,700-$3,000

"Poesie D'Orsay"
a perfume bottle for D'Orsay, in clear and frosted
glass with sepia patina, circa 1914, 5 3/4" tall. (M p.
934, D'Orsay 8)

$1,500+

"Quatre Soleils"
in satin glass with sepia patina, circa 1912, 3" tall. (M p. 333, No. 505)

$3,000+

"Quatre Cigales"
in clear and frosted glass with sepia patina, circa 1910, 5
1/8" tall. (M p. 325, No. 475)

$2,000+

"Quelques Fleurs"
a perfume bottle for Houbigant, in clear and frosted glass, circa 1928, 2 1/8" tall. (M p. 941, Houbigant 7)

$600+ (undamaged)

Perfume Containers

"Raquette"
a perfume bottle for Worth, in clear glass with blue enamel detailing, in original, unopened condition, stenciled LALIQUE, 6 1/4" tall. (M p. 934, No. 25)
$1,000-$1,200

"Raquette"
a perfume bottle for Worth, designed 1944, this example circa 1949, in clear glass with blue enamel, unopened, complete with original contents and card display box, stenciled LALIQUE FRANCE, bottle 6 1/4" tall. (M p. 954, No. 25)
$900-$1,100

"Relief"
a perfume bottle for Forvil, circa 1924, in clear glass, molded R. LALIQUE PARIS FRANCE, 5 1/2" tall. (M p. 938, No. 7)
$400-$500

"Requette"
a perfume bottle for Worth, in clear glass with blue enamel decoration, with original box, circa 1944; in two sizes, 3" and 3 1/1/2" tall. (M p. 954, Worth 26)
$600+

"Requette"
a perfume bottle for Worth, in clear glass with blue enamel decoration, and original box, circa 1944, in sizes ranging from 6 1/3" to 10 7/8" tall. (M p. 954, Worth 25)
$600+

"Rosace Figurines"
a perfume bottle, circa 1912, figural stopper version, in clear and frosted glass with sepia patina, engraved R. Lalique France, 4 1/2" tall. (M p. 327, No. 488)
$3,800-$4,200

"Requette"
a perfume bottle for Worth, in clear glass with blue enamel decoration, circa 1944, in sizes ranging from 6 1/3" to 10 7/8v tall. (M p. 954, Worth 25)
$700+

"Requette"
a perfume bottle for Worth, in clear glass with blue enamel decoration, circa 1944; in two sizes, 3" and 3 1/1/2" tall. (M p. 954, Worth 26)
$400+

"Rosace Figurines"
in opalescent glass, circa 1912, 4 1/3" tall. (M p. 327, No. 488) (Also found with gold or silver patina, and with figural stopper.)
$2,500+

Perfume Containers

"Roses"
a clear and frosted glass perfume bottle for
D'Orsay, circa 1912, molded LALIQUE, 4" tall. (M
p. 933, No. 3)

$2,700-$3,200

"Rose Sans Fin"
two perfume bottles for Arys, circa 1919, in clear and frosted glass, molded R. LALIQUE ARYS, taller 3 1/2".
(M p. 923, No. 5)

$300-$400/pair

"Roses"
a perfume bottle for D'Orsay, circa 1912, in clear
and frosted glass, molded LALIQUE with extended
L, 4" tall. (M p. 933, No. 3)

$2,300-$2,500

"Salamandres"
in clear and frosted glass, circa 1914, 3 3/4" tall. (M p. 328, No. 491)

$2,800+

"Sans Adieu"
a perfume bottle for Worth, in teal green glass, and with monogrammed stopper used after 1929, in sizes ranging from 3 1/8" to 9 1/1/2" tall. (M p. 953, Worth 13)

$900+

"Sans Adieu"
a lotion bottle for Worth, in green glass, circa 1929, in sizes ranging from 1/2" to 5 7/8" tall. (M p. 952, Worth 12)

$700+

"Sans Adieu"
two sizes of perfume bottles for Worth, in teal green glass, circa 1929, 4 1/1/2" and 5 1/3" tall. (M p. 952, Worth 11)

$600-$800

"Satyre"
in clear and frosted glass, circa 1933, 3 1/1/2" tall. (M p. 338, No. 527)

$3,500+

Perfume Containers

"Styx"
a perfume bottle for Coty, in clear and frosted glass, circa 1912, 4 3/4" tall. (M p. 928, Coty 16)

$700+

"Serpent"
"Serpent," in clear and frosted glass with gray patina, circa 1920, 3 1/1/2" tall. (M p. 331, No. 502)

$1,200-$1,500

"Styx"
a perfume bottle for Coty, in clear and frosted glass with sepia patina, molded LALIQUE, stopper frozen. (M p. 928, No. 16)

$900-$1,000

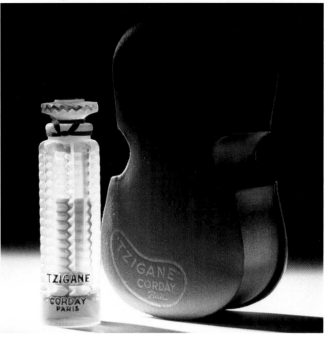

"Telline"

a perfume bottle, circa 1920, in clear and frosted glass with gray patina, engraved R. Lalique France, No. 508, 3 3/4" tall. (M p. 333, No. 508)

$750-$850

"Tzigane"

a perfume bottle for Corday, in clear and frosted glass with black enamel detailing, together with original magenta silk and gilt card violin-form display box, molded R. LALIQUE, box 6 1/4" tall. (M p. 926, Corday 1)

$500-$600

"Vase Deux Anemones"

in clear and frosted glass with black enamel decoration, circa 1935, 6 1/4" tall. (M p. 339, No. 530)

$1,500+

"Vers La Jour"

a perfume bottle for Worth, in deep amber glass, circa 1926, in sizes ranging from 3" to 6" tall. (M p. 952, Worth 6)

$800-$1,200

Perfume Containers
Perfume Bottle Sets

Three perfume bottles
for Worth Fragrances, 1930s, comprising one "Vers Toi" and two "En Croisiere," all sealed and with original contents, all molded R. LALIQUE, tallest 3 1/2". (M pp. 953 and 954)
$600-$700/set

Three perfume bottles
circa 1970, in clear and frosted glass, comprising "Enfantes" (mid-size), "Dahlias" (small-size), and "Deux Fleurs," all engraved Lalique France.
$500-$550/set

Three perfume bottles
in clear glass, 1920s, comprising "Pavots D'Argent" for Roger et Gallet, "Chypre" for Forvil, and "Chypre" for D'Orsay, all molded R. LALIQUE, tallest 2 3/4". (M pp. 937, 938, and 949)
$750-$850/set

A set of three perfume bottles
for Worth Fragrance, in clear glass, all molded R. LALIQUE, tallest 5". (M p. 954, No. 22)
$800-$900/set

Five perfume bottles
most 1930s, comprising large and small "Tzigane" for Corday with enameled lettering, a pair of clear bottles "Je Reviens" for Worth, all molded R. LALIQUE, together with a modern "L'Air Du Temps" for Nina Ricci, tallest 6 3/4".
$700-$800/set

Perfume Containers

Five perfume bottles
for Worth Fragrances, 1930s, comprising one "Vers Toi" and two "Imprudence," in clear glass, and two blue Art Deco bottles for "Je Reviens," all molded R. LALIQUE, tallest 5". (M pp. 953 and 954)

$800-$900/set

A group of six perfume bottles
for Nina Ricci, circa 1960-1980, in clear and frosted glass, comprising five single and one double dove examples, all sealed and with original contents, tallest 4 1/2".

$500-$600/set

Perfume Accessories

"La Renommee D'Orsay"
a perfume tester for D'Orsay, in clear and frosted glass with sepia patina, molded LALIQUE. (M p. 935, No. 21)

$3,000-$3,500

"Danseuses Egyptiennes"
a perfume burner, circa 1926, in clear glass, with black enamel highlights and chrome fittings, original wick, molded R. LALIQUE FRANCE, 5 1/4" tall. (M p. 962, No. 1)

$500-$600

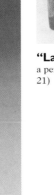

"Quatvre Flacons"
a perfume presentation for Houbigant, circa 1928, comprising four bottles fitted in an opalescent glass and clear glass and satin box, lacking stoppers, 5 1/4" diameter. (M p. 969, No. 2)

$600-$700

Plates, also see "Tableware"

"Calypso"
a plate, in clear and frosted glass, circa 1930, 14 1/8"
diameter. (M p. 301, No. 413)

$2,700+

"Calypso"
a plate, in opalescent glass, circa 1930, 14 1/8" diameter. (M p. 301, No. 413)

$5,800+

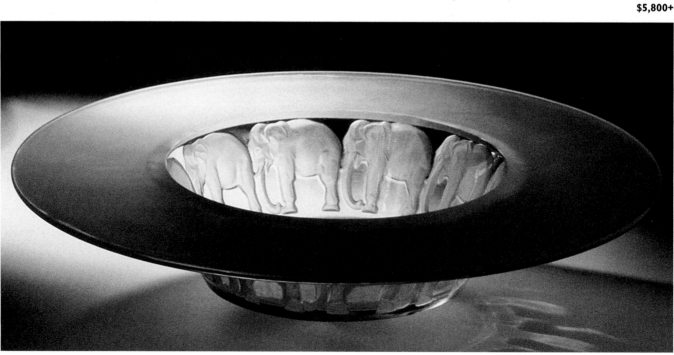

"Elephants"
a wide shallow bowl, in clear and frosted glass, circa 1930, 15 1/8" diameter. (M p. 300, No. 411)

$10,000-$15,000

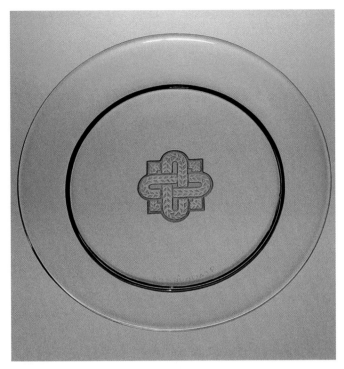

"Molsheim"
a dessert plate, in clear and frosted glass, circa 1931, 8 1/1/2"
diameter. (M p. 706, No. 3043)

$200+

"Martigues"
a plate, in butterscotch amber glass, circa 1920, 14 1/8" diameter. (M p. 290, No. 377)

$2,000+

"Poissons No. 1"
a shallow plate, in opalescent glass, circa 1931, 11 7/8" diameter. (M p. 758, No. 3263)

$3,000+

Tableware

Vintage Lalique tableware—even stylish art deco examples from the 1930s—can still be found for a few hundred dollars. Careful attention must be paid to condition. It is common to find rims and bases ground or polished to remove nicks and flakes.

"Cannes"
set of six LALIQUE Bourdeaux glasses, circa 1938, stenciled R. LALIQUE FRANCE, 7 7/8" tall. (M p. 856, No. 5396)

$800-$900/set

"Molsheim" tableware
goblets and carafe, clear and frosted glass, circa 1924. (M p. 830)

$200-$400 each

"Coqs et Raisins"
a cocktail shaker, in clear and frosted glass with sepia patina, circa 1928, 8 7/8" tall. (M p. 813, No. 3879)

$5,000+

"Hortense"

a cake tray, circa 1942, in clear and frosted glass with engraved decoration, molded R. LALIQUE, 15 1/3" diameter. (M p. 821, No. 3918)

$400-$500

"Champagne Ange"

a set of six champagne glasses in the Angel design, modern, in original box, engraved Lalique France in script, 8" tall.

$1,000-$1,200/set

"Masques"

a carafe, circa 1913, in clear and frosted glass with sepia patina, engraved R. Lalique France, 9 7/8" tall. (M p. 738, No. 3156)

$1,800-$2,200

"William"

a cocktail glass, circa 1925, in clear and frosted glass with blue enameled details, engraved R. Lalique France, 6 5/8" tall. (M p. 808, No. 3672)

$400-$500

"Satyr"

a carafe, circa 1923, in clear and frosted glass with sepia patina, engraved R. Lalique pour Cusenier, 10 1/4" tall. The mark indicates this is one of a group sold through the wine merchant Cusenier in the 1920s. (M p. 741, No. 3167)

$2,400-$2,800

Tableware

"Bahia"
a cold drinks service, circa 1931, in amber glass, with jug, six tumblers and tray, all stenciled R. LALIQUE FRANCE, jug 9" tall. (M p. 798, No. 3683)

$2,800-$3,200/set

"Blidah"
a cold drinks service, circa 1931, in amber glass, with jug and six tumblers, together with a complimentary tray in the "Setubal" pattern, all stenciled R. LALIQUE FRANCE, jug 8" tall. (M p. 797, No. 3681, and p. 799, No. 3684)

$2,000-$2,500/set

"Flora-Bella"
a coupe (shallow bowl with broad rim), circa 1930, in clear and opalescent glass, stenciled R. LALIQUE FRANCE, 15 1/2" diameter. (M p. 299, No. 407)

$2,700-$3,000

"Selestat"
a decanter and stopper, circa 1925, in clear glass with applied black glass ring at the neck, molded R. LALIQUE FRANCE, 11" tall. (M p. 834, No. 5072)

$1,700-$2,000

"Gui"
a coupe (shallow bowl with broad rim), in clear glass with green patina, wheel-cut R. LALIQUE FRANCE, 9 1/4" diameter. (M p. 751, No. 3224)

$450-$550

"Nippon"
a decanter set with six glasses, in clear glass, decanter stenciled R. LALIQUE FRANCE, glasses R. Lalique France in script, decanter 10" tall. (M p. 443, No. 3173)

$1,100-$1,400/set

"Vigne Strie"
a decanter and pair of wine glasses, circa 1920, in clear and frosted glass with sepia patina, molded LALIQUE on stopper, decanter 11 3/8" tall. (M p. 835)

$1,200-$1,600/set

"Dauphines"
a shallow dish, circa 1932, in opalescent glass with sepia patina, stenciled R. LALIQUE FRANCE, 11 1/4" diameter. (M p. 307, No. 10-304)

$900-$1,100

"Epines"
a drinks tray, circa 1920, in clear and frosted glass, molded R. LALIQUE, 11 7/8" diameter. (M p. 793, No. 3671)

$350-$400

"Muguet"
a shallow dish, circa 1931, in opalescent glass, stenciled R. LALIQUE FRANCE, 11 7/8" diameter. (M p. 302, No. 416)

$1,800-$2,000

"Bahia"
a pair of fruit juice glasses, circa 1931, in orange glass with sepia patina, stenciled R. LALIQUE, 5" tall. (M p. 798, No. 3683)

$250-$300/pair

"Blidah"
a pair of fruit juice glasses, circa 1931, in orange glass with sepia patina, stenciled R. LALIQUE, 5 1/8" tall. (M p. 797, No. 3681)

$250-$300/pair

Tableware

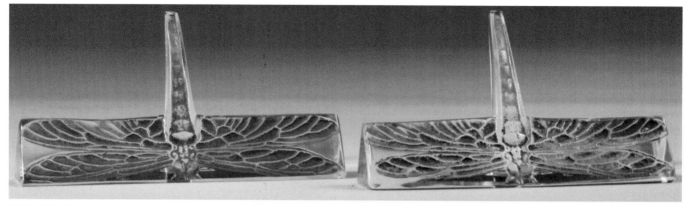

"Libellule"

a pair of knife rests, circa 1919, in clear and frosted glass with gray patina, engraved R. Lalique, 3 3/4" long, some edges polished. (M p. 787, No. 3602)

$800-$900/pair

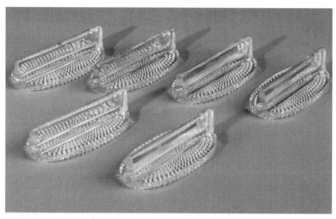

"Nippon"

set of six clear glass knife rests, stenciled R. LALIQUE, 3 1/2" long. (M p. 788, No. 3605)

$450-$550/set

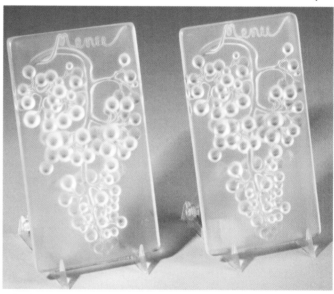

"Raisin Muscat"

a pair of menu plaques, circa 1924, in clear and frosted glass, both engraved R. Lalique France, 6" tall. (M p. 794, No. 3475)

$850-$950/pair

"Enfants"

a set of six liqueur glasses, designed 1937, these examples circa 1955, in clear and frosted glass with sepia patina, one repaired, stenciled LALIQUE CRYSTAL FRANCE, 1 1/2" tall. (M p. 770, No. 3418)

$800-$900/set

"Pinsons"

a pair of menu holders, circa 1924, in clear and frosted glass, both engraved R. Lalique France, 1 3/4" tall. (M p. 784, No. 3501)

$550-$650/pair

"Bourgeuil"

a modern oil and vinegar cruet together with a modern footed vase, both engraved Lalique France, vase 5 3/4" tall.

$400-$500/pair

"Hesperides" and "Bahia,"
a pitcher and a serving tray, both circa 1931, in orange glass, both stenciled R. LALIQUE, pitcher 8 5/8" tall. (M p. 798, Nos. 3682 and 3683)

$800-$900/pair

"Coquilles No. 2"
a plate, circa 1930, in opalescent glass, 10 1/2" diameter. (M p. 701, No. 3010)

$750-$850

"Fleurons No. 2"
a plate, in opalescent glass, stenciled R. LALIQUE FRANCE, 10 1/2" diameter. (M p. 722, No. 10-3043)

$350-$400

"Algues"
a plate, circa 1933, in opalescent glass, wheel-cut R. LALIQUE FRANCE, 14" diameter. (M p. 308, No. 10-390)

$700-$800

"Coquilles"
a plate, circa 1930, in opalescent glass, 9 1/8" diameter. (M p. 701, No. 3011)

$500-$600

"Ondes"
a plate, circa 1935, in opalescent glass, stenciled R. Lalique France, 10 7/8" diameter. (M p. 721, No. 10-3035)

$800-$900

Tableware

"Ondines"
a plate, circa 1921, in opalescent glass, wheel-cut R. LALIQUE FRANCE, engraved No. 3003, 11" diameter. (M p. 699, No. 3003)

$1,700-$1,900

"Vases"
two plates, circa 1921, in clear and frosted glass with sepia and gray patina, 8 1/2" diameter. (M p. 753, No. 3233)

$400-$450/pair

"Volutes"
a plate, circa 1928, in opalescent glass, stenciled R. LALIQUE, 10 5/8" diameter. (M p. 310, No. 10-396)

$700-$800

"Hagueneau"
a set of 12 red wine glasses, circa 1924, in clear glass, stenciled or engraved R. LALIQUE FRANCE, 7 1/2" tall. (M p. 829, No. 5022)

$2,200-$2,600/set

"Epis"
a service plate, circa 1921, in clear and frosted glass with green patina, stenciled R. LALIQUE FRANCE, 11 5/8" diameter. (M p. 753, No. 3235)

$350-$450

"Pissenlit"
a service plate and side dishes, circa 1921, in clear and frosted glass with green patina, stenciled R. LALIQUE, plate 9 3/8" diameter. (M p. 750, No. 3215)

$600-$700/set

"Algues"
a serving plate, circa 1933, in opalescent glass, stenciled R. LALIQUE FRANCE, 15 3/4" diameter. (M p. 308, No.10-390)

$550-$650

"Bulbes No. 2"
a serving plate, in clear glass, stenciled R. LALIQUE FRANCE. (M p. 722, No. 10-3037.)

$300-$350

"Ecailles"
a serving plate, circa 1928, in clear glass, stenciled R. LALIQUE FRANCE, 12 1/2" diameter. (M p. 754, No. 3027)

$175-$225

Tableware

Three table articles
circa 1925-50: a bowl, "Thionville" pattern with black enamel highlights; a water goblet, "Reims" pattern; and a salad plate, circa 1950, various marks. (M pp. 730, 845)

$150-$200/set

"Laure"
a black glass serving plate, circa 1970, the border patterned with waves, engraved Lalique France, 10 7/8" long.

$350-$450

"Anenome Ferme" and "Anenome Ouverte"
a pair of table ornaments, circa 1931, in clear and frosted glass with black enamel highlights, stenciled R. LALIQUE, each 4" long. (M p. 488, Nos. 1179 and 1180)

$400-$450/pair

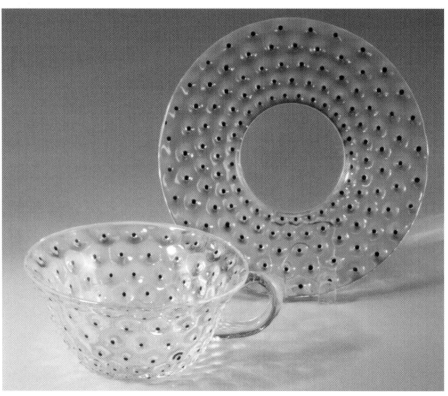

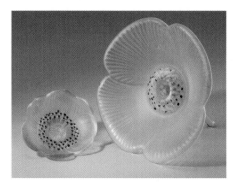

"Pavot"
a table ornament, circa 1928, in clear and frosted glass with black enamel highlights, together with "Anenome Ferme," 1931, stenciled R. LALIQUE, larger 6 1/2" diameter. (M p. 475, H, and p. 488, No. 1180)

$250-$350/pair

"Cactus"
a teacup and saucer, circa 1933, in clear glass with black enamel highlights, stenciled R. LALIQUE, saucer 4 3/4" diameter. (M p. 819, Nos. 3096 and 3907)

$500-$600/pair

"Reims"
a set of 10 water goblets, circa 1942, in clear and frosted glass, the base with a zigzag frieze, stenciled R. LALIQUE FRANCE, 5" tall. (M p. 771, No. 3426)

$1,000-$1,200/set

"Hagueneau"
set of four white wine glasses, circa 1924, in clear and frosted glass, stenciled R. LALIQUE FRANCE. (M p. 829)

$300-$350/set

"Roxanne"
a set of 12 modern wine glasses, circa 1980, six red and six white, in clear and frosted glass, all engraved Lalique France.

$900-$1,100/set

"Monogramme"
a wine glass, circa 1924, in clear glass, with black enamel monogram "SH," 5" tall. (M p. 831, No. 5045) This example was produced by Rene Lalique for the wedding of his daughter, Suzanne, to Paul Haviland in 1924.

$1,500-$2,000

"Epernay"
a wine cooler, circa 1938, in clear and frosted glass, stenciled R. LALIQUE FRANCE, 7 3/8" tall. (M p. 802, No. 3730)

$1,200-$1,500

"Malaga"
a wine rinse, designed 1937, this example circa 1950, in clear and frosted glass, engraved Lalique France, 5 3/4" tall. (M p. 782, No. 10-3475)

$275-$325

"Sarment"
a wine rinse, in opalescent glass, stenciled R. LALIQUE FRANCE. (M p. 782, No. 10-3478.)

$900-$1,000

Vases

Lalique's genius for design reaches its height in the vases he created for nearly three decades. From the sinuous art-nouveau-influenced gourds and vines of "Courges," to the stately budgerigars of "Ceylan," and the regal prancing horse of "Camargue," it seemed there was no facet of the natural world that Lalique couldn't transform into vessels of color and light that are anything but utilitarian.

"Acacia"
in clear and frosted glass with charcoal gray patina, engraved R. Lalique France, 7 7/8" tall. (M p. 428, No. 949)

$800-$900

"Acacia"
circa 1921, in topaz glass, molded R. LALIQUE, 7 7/8" tall. (M p. 428, No. 949)

$900-$1,100

"Acanthes"
circa 1921, in blue glass, 11 1/1/2" tall. (M p. 417, No. 902)

$12,000+

"Acanthes"
circa 1921, extremely rare in cased butterscotch glass, 11 1/4" tall. (M p. 417, No. 902)

$20,000

Vases

"Acanthes"
circa 1921, in red glass, 11 1/1/2" tall. (M p. 417, No. 902)

$15,000+

"Acanthes"
circa 1921, in clear and frosted glass, 11 1/1/2" tall. (M p. 417, No. 902)

$3,000+

"Acanthes"
circa 1922, extremely rare in pink glass, 11 1/2"
tall. (M p. 417, No. 902)

$22,000+

Vases

"Actina"
circa 1934, in clear and frosted glass with blue patina, stenciled R. LALIQUE FRANCE, 8 5/8" tall. (M p. 462, No. 10-889)

$1,200-$1,400

"Aigrettes"
in iridescent green glass, circa 1926, 10 1/8" tall. (M p. 436, No. 988)

$7,000+

"Aigrettes"
in topaz glass, circa 1926, 10 1/8" tall. (M p. 436, No. 988)

$4,000+

"Aigrettes"
in deep purple glass, circa 1926, 10 1/8" tall. (M p. 436, No. 988)

$6,000+

"Albert"
circa 1925,
in deep topaz
glass, wheel-cut
R. LALIQUE,
engraved
France, 6 3/4"
tall. (M p. 430,
No. 958)
$2,200-$2,600

"Albert"
circa 1925, in blue
glass, wheel-cut R.
LALIQUE, engraved
France, 6 3/4" tall. (M
p. 430, No. 958)
$4,000+

"Alicante"
circa 1928, in
triple-cased lime
green glass, wheel-
cut R. Lalique
France in script,
10 1/4" tall. (M p.
438, No. 998)
$15,000+

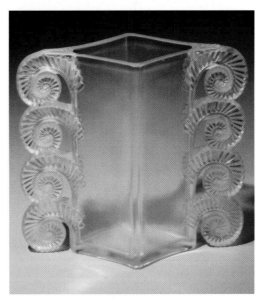

"Amiens"
circa 1929, in
opalescent glass,
wheel-cut R
LALIQUE, 7 1/4"
tall. (M p. 443,
No. 1023)
$1,700-$2,000

"Annecy"
circa 1935, in clear glass
with black enameled
highlights, stenciled R.
LALIQUE FRANCE, 6" tall.
(M p. 461, No. 10-884)
$1,500-$1,600

Vases

"Aras"
circa 1924, in clear and frosted glass with
blue patina, molded R. LALIQUE, 8 1/4" tall.
(M p. 421, No. 919)
$2,500-$2,700

"Aras"
circa 1924, in blue green glass, molded R. LALIQUE, 9 3/8" tall. (M p. 421, No. 919)
$6,000+

"Aras"
circa 1924, in iridescent teal green glass with white patina, molded R. LALIQUE, 9 3/8" tall. (M p. 421, No. 919)
$8,000+

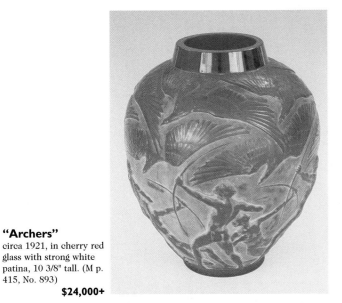

"Archers"
circa 1921, in cherry red
glass with strong white
patina, 10 3/8" tall. (M p.
415, No. 893)

$24,000+

"Archers"
circa 1921, in
electric blue glass
with traces of white
patina, molded R.
Lalique, 10 1/2" tall.
(M p. 415, No. 893)

$22,000+

"Archers"
circa 1921, in cased
butterscotch yellow
glass, engraved Lalique,
10 1/4" tall. (M p. 415,
No. 893)

$18,000-$22,000

"Archers"
circa 1921, in
clear and frosted
glass with blue
patina, molded R.
LALIQUE, 10 1/4"
tall. (M p. 415, No.
893)

$4,800-$5,200

"Archers"
in black glass, circa
1921, 10 3/8" tall. (M p.
415, No. 893)

$10,000+

"Archers"
in deep amber glass,
engraved R. Lalique
France No. 993, 10
1/4" tall. (Ref. M p.
415, No. 993)

$8,000-$10,000

Vases

"Avalon"
circa 1927, in clear and frosted glass, wheel-cut R. LALIQUE FRANCE, 5 3/4"
tall. (M p. 436, No. 986)

$1,200-$1,400

"Avalon"
circa 1935, in opalescent glass, stenciled R. LALIQUE FRANCE, 5 3/4" tall. (M
p. 436, No. 986)

$1,600-$1,700

"Avalon"
circa 1927, in topaz glass, wheel-cut R. LALIQUE FRANCE, 5 3/4" tall. (M p.
436, No. 986)

$1,700-$2,000

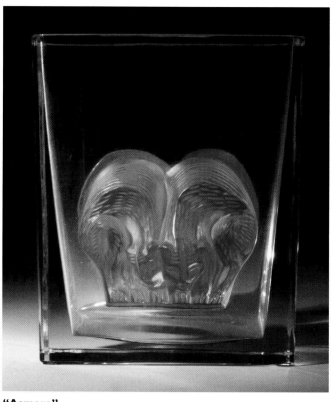

"Asmara"
modern (discontinued), decorated with cats in opalescent amber and clear
glass, engraved Lalique France, 6 3/4" tall.

$700-$800

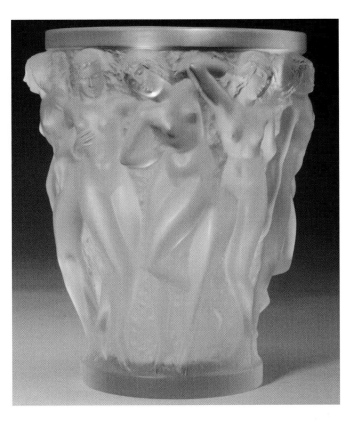

"Bacchantes"
circa 1960, in clear and frosted glass, stenciled LALIQUE CRYSTAL FRANCE.
$2,000-$2,300

"Bacchantes"
in topaz glass, with original (?) display stand, circa 1927, vase 9 7/8" tall. (M p. 438, No. 997)
$15,000+

"Bacchantes"
in opalescent glass, with original (?) display stand, circa 1927, vase 9 7/8" tall. (M p. 438, No. 997)
$35,000+

"Bagatelle" and "Pinsons"
a vase and a fruit bowl, circa 1955, in clear and frosted glass, both engraved LALIQUE FRANCE.
$450-$500/pair

Vases

"Baies"
in satin glass with black enamel, circa 1924, 10 3/8" tall. (M p. 416, No. 894)

$8,000+

"Bandes des Roses"
circa 1919, in clear and frosted glass with sepia patina, molded R. LALIQUE with extended L, 9 1/2" tall. (M p. 419, No. 910)

$1,700-$1,800

"Beautrellis"
circa 1927, in topaz glass, wheel-cut R. LALIQUE FRANCE, 5 1/2" tall. (M p. 436, No. 989)

$1,500-$1,700

"Beaulieu"
in blue glass, circa 1925, 6 3/4" tall. (M p. 430, No. 960)

$2,000+

"Beaulieu"
in topaz glass, circa 1925, 6 3/4" tall. (M p. 430, No. 960)

$1,500

"Beliers"
a vase in cobalt blue glass, circa 1925, 7 1/1/2" tall. (M p. 418, No. 904)

$5,000+

"Bellecour"
in clear and frosted glass, circa 1927, 11 1/8" tall. (M p. 437, No. 993)

$25,000+

"Biches"
circa 1932, in clear and frosted glass with sepia patina, engraved R. Lalique France, 6 1/2" tall. (M p. 456, No. 1082)

$700-$800

"Bordure Epines"
in clear and frosted glass with gray patina, wheel-cut LALIQUE FRANCE. (Ref. M p. 418, No. 908)

$1,700-$2,000

"Borneo"
circa 1930, in clear and frosted glass with blue enameled highlights, wheel-cut R. LALIQUE FRANCE, 9" tall. (M p. 450, No. 1056)

$2,000-$2,500

"Borrome"
circa 1928, in clear and frosted glass with sepia patina, engraved R. Lalique France, 9" tall. (M p. 422, No. 1017)

$2,300-$2,800

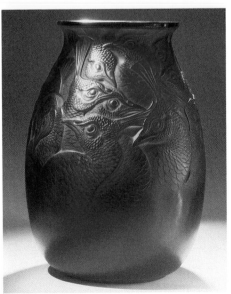

"Bouchardon"
circa 1926, in clear and frosted glass with sepia patina, molded R. LALIQUE, 4 3/4" tall. (M p. 435, No. 981)

$2,500-$3,000

"Borrome"
circa 1928, in peacock blue glass vase with white patina, stenciled R. LALIQUE, 9" tall. (Ref. M p. 442, No. 1017)

$7,000-$8,000

Vases

"Bresse"
in deep red glass with white patina, circa 1931, 4 1/8" tall. (M p. 454, No. 1073)
$10,000+

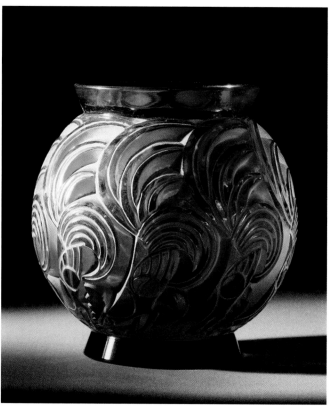

"Bresse"
in deep amber glass, circa 1931, 4 1/8" tall. (M p. 454, No. 1073)
$6,000+

"Bresse"
in cased opalescent glass with green patina, circa 1931, 4 1/8" tall. (M p. 454, No. 1073)
$5,000+

"Camaret"
in opalescent glass, circa 1928, engraved R. Lalique France No. 1010, 6 3/4" tall. (M p. 441, No.1010)
$1.600+

"Carmargue"
circa 1942, in clear and frosted glass, engraved Lalique France, base with large polished area, 11 5/8" tall. (M p. 742, No. 10-937)

$1,900-$2,300

"Camargue"
circa 1943, in clear and frosted glass with sepia patina, engraved Lalique France, 11" tall. (M p. 472, No. 10-937)

$4,000-$4,500

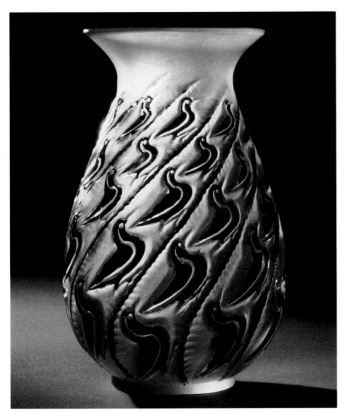

"Canards"
in satin glass, circa 1931, 5 1/3" tall. (M p. 455, No. 1076)

$1,000+

"Carthage"
in cobalt blue glass with white patina, circa 1930, 7 1/8" tall. (M p. 449, No. 1051)

$4,000+

Vases

"Cerises"
in clear and frosted glass, circa 1930, 7 7/8" tall.
(M p. 446, No. 1035)

$3,000+

"Cerises"
circa 1930, in opalescent glass with blue patina,
stenciled R. LALIQUE FRANCE, 7 7/8" tall. (M p.
446, No. 1035)

$3,000-$3,500

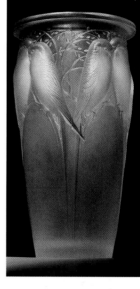

"Ceylan"
circa 1924,
in opalescent
glass, wheel-cut
R. LALIQUE
FRANCE, 9 1/2"
tall. (M p. 418,
No. 905)
$5,500-$6,000

"Ceylan"
circa 1924,
in opalescent
glass with blue
patina, wheel-
cut R. LALIQUE
FRANCE, 9 7/8"
tall. (M p. 418,
No. 905)
$7,000-$7,500

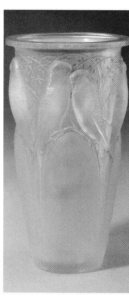

"Ceylan"
a vase, in
opalescent
glass with gray
patina, wheel-
cut LALIQUE
FRANCE, 9 1/2"
tall. (Ref. M p.
418, No. 905)
$5,000-$6,000

"Ceylan"
in opalescent
glass with sepia
patina, wheel-
cut LALIQUE
FRANCE, 9 1/2"
tall. (M p. 418,
No. 905)
$7,000-$8,000

"Chamois"
circa 1931, in
clear and frosted
glass with blue
patina, stenciled
R. LALIQUE
FRANCE, 5" tall.
(M p. 455, No.
1075)
$800-$900

"Chamois"
in opalescent yellow
glass, circa 1931, 5"
tall. (M p. 455, No.
1075)

$3,000+

"Chardons"
circa 1922, in clear and frosted glass, engraved R. Lalique France, 7 7/8" tall.
(M p. 423, No. 929)

$700-$800

"Chardons"
in amber glass, circa 1922, 7 7/8 in. tall. (M p. 423, No. 929)

$2,500+

"Chataignier"
circa 1933, in clear and frosted glass, stenciled R. LALIQUE FRANCE, 5" tall.
(M p. 458, No. 1092)

$350-$450

"Coqs et Plumes"
circa 1928, in clear and frosted glass, wheel-cut R. LALIQUE FRANCE, 6" tall.
(M p. 445, No. 1033)

$800-$900

Vases

"Coq et Raisins"
circa 1928, in clear and frosted glass with blue-gray patina, stenciled R. LALIQUE FRANCE, 6 1/8" tall. (M p. 446, No. 1034)

$1,000-$1,200

"Coquilles"
circa 1920, in clear and frosted glass, molded R. LALIQUE, 7 1/2" tall. (M p. 424, No. 932)

$400-$500

"Chamonix"
circa 1933, in opalescent glass, stenciled R. LALIQUE FRANCE, 6" tall. (M p. 458, No. 1090)

$900-$1,000

"Champagne"
circa 1927, in topaz glass, engraved R. Lalique France, 6 1/8" tall. (M p. 439, No. 1004)

$1,700-$1,900

"Courges"
circa 1914, in electric blue glass with white patina, molded R. Lalique, 7 7/8" tall. (M p. 417, No. 900)

$9,000-$11,000

"Courges"
circa 1914, in cobalt blue glass with traces of white patina, molded R. Lalique, 7 7/8" tall. (M p. 417, No. 900)

$9,000-$11,000

"Cyrus"
modern (discontinued), in clear and turquoise glass, engraved Lalique France, 6" tall.

$1,200-$1,400

"Cytise"
in opalescent glass, circa 1926, 5 1/8" tall. (M p. 458, No. 1095)

$1,000+

"Dahlias"
in clear and frosted glass with black enameled detail, stenciled R. Lalique, 5" tall. (Ref. M p. 425, No. 938)

$1,500-$1,800

"Dahlias"
circa 1919, in clear and frosted glass with sepia patina and black enamel highlights, engraved R. Lalique France, No. 928, 5" tall. (M p. 425, No. 938)

$2,400-$2,600

"Dahlias"
circa 1925, in clear and frosted glass, with silver metal rim, gray patina and black enamel, molded R. LALIQUE, 5 1/2" tall. (M p. 425, No. 938)

$1,800-$2,000

Vases

A pair of modern "Dampierre" vases
both engraved R. Lalique France.

$400-$450/pair

"Dauphins"
circa 1932, in opalescent glass with blue patina, stenciled R
LALIQUE FRANCE, 6" tall. (M p. 464, No. 10-900)

$2,200-$2,400

"Davos"
circa 1932, in amber glass, engraved R. Lalique, 11 1/2" tall. (M p. 455, No.
1079)

$3,500-$4,000

"Davos"
in opalescent glass, stenciled R. Lalique France, 11 1/2" tall. (Ref. M p. 455, No.
1079)

$2,200-$2,500

"Deauville"
designed 1942, this example circa 1948, in clear and frosted glass, together with a modern vase, circa 1960, in clear and frosted glass, stenciled LALIQUE FRANCE marks, taller 9 7/8". (M p. 471, No. 10-935)
$225-$275/pair

"Dentele"
circa 1912, in clear and frosted glass with gray patina, stenciled R. LALIQUE, engraved France, 6 3/4" tall. (M p. 426, No. 943)
$700-$800

"Daimers"
in clear and frosted glass with black enamel decoration, wide foot, circa 1935, 8 7/8 in. tall. (M p. 462, No. 10-866)
$4,000+

"Dauphins"
circa 1932, in opalescent glass with blue patina, stenciled R LALIQUE FRANCE, 5 1/2" tall. (M p. 464, No. 10-900)
$2,200-$2,400

"Daimers"
in clear and frosted glass with black enamel decoration, narrow foot, circa 1935, 8 3/8" tall. (M p. 462, No. 10-866)
$3,000+

Vases

"Domremy"
in iridescent green
glass with white
patina, circa 1926, 8
5/8" tall. (M p. 434,
No. 979)

$7,000+

"Domremy"
circa 1926, in cased
opalescent glass with
blue patina, molded R.
LALIQUE, 8 5/8" tall.
(M p. 434, No. 979)

$1,400-$1,600

"Domremy"
in cased opalescent glass with sepia patina,
stenciled R. LALIQUE, engraved France, 8 1/2" tall.
(Ref. M p. 434, No. 979)

$2,200-$2,500

"Domremy"
circa 1926, in clear and frosted glass, molded R.
LALIQUE, engraved France, 8 1/4" tall. (M p. 434,
No. 979)

$850-$950

"Domremy"
circa 1926, in deep amber glass, engraved R.
Lalique France No. 979, 8 5/8" tall. (M p. 434, No.
979)

$2,400-$2,600

"Domremy"
circa 1926, in
opalescent glass with
sepia patina, engraved
R. Lalique France No.
979, 8 1/2" tall. (M p.
434, No. 979)

$1,700-$1,800

"Domremy"
circa 1926, in topaz
glass with sepia
patina, stenciled R.
LALIQUE, 8 1/2" tall.
(M p. 434, No. 979)

$2,400-$2,600

"Dordogne"
circa 1927, in white opalescent glass with sepia patina, molded R. LALIQUE, engraved R. Lalique France, 7 1/8" tall. (M p. 439, No. 1001)

$6,000-$7,000

"Douze Figurines Avec Bouchon Figure"
vase with stopper, circa 1920, in clear and frosted glass, engraved R. Lalique France No. 914, 11 1/2" tall. (M p. 420, No. 914)

$3,200-$3,400

"Druides"
in cased opalescent glass with green patina, molded R. LALIQUE, 7" tall. (M p. 425, No. 937)

$2,000-$2,300

"Druides"
circa 1924, in opalescent glass with green patina, molded R. LALIQUE, 7" tall. (M p. 425, No. 937)

$1,400-$1,600

"Druides"
circa 1924, in opalescent glass with green patina, engraved R. Lalique France, 7 1/2" tall. (M p. 424, No. 937)

$1,700-$1,900

"Ecailles"
circa 1932, in deep topaz glass, stenciled R. LALIQUE FRANCE, 9 3/4" tall. (M p. 456, No. 1080)

$3,400-$4,000

"Ecailles"
in cased red glass, circa 1932, stenciled R. LALIQUE FRANCE, 9 7/8" tall. (M p. 456, No. 1080)

$7,000+

Vases

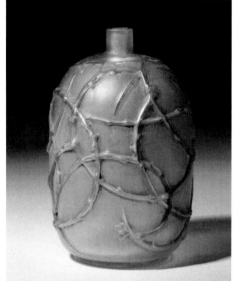

"Eglantines"
circa 1921, in clear
and frosted glass with
gray patina, engraved
R. Lalique, 4 3/4" tall.
(M p. 429, No. 954)

$400-$500

"Eglantines"
circa 1921, in
opalescent glass,
stenciled R. LALIQUE
FRANCE, 4 3/4" tall.
(M p. 429, No. 954)

$600-$700

**A pair of
modern
"Elisabeth"
vases**
Both engraved R.
Lalique France.

$500-$600/pair

"Epicea"
circa 1923,
in clear and
frosted glass
with gray
patina, molded
R. LALIQUE,
wheel-cut
FRANCE, 9"
tall. (M p. 421,
No. 921)

$900-$1,100

**Three modern
vases**
including "Ermenonville,"
"Lucie," and "Deux
Tulipes." All engraved
Lalique France, tallest 6".

$300-$350/set

"Escargot"
in blue glass, circa
1920, 8 5/8" tall. (M p.
424, No. 931)

$12,000+

"Espalion"
in opalescent glass
with blue gray patina,
molded R. LALIQUE,
engraved France, 7"
tall. (M p. 438, No.
996)

$1,500-$1,800

"Escargot"
in dark red glass, circa
1920, 8 5/8" tall. (M p.
424, No. 931)

$15,000+

"Espalion"
circa 1927, in
opalescent glass with
blue patina, molded R.
LALIQUE, 7" tall. (M
p. 438, No. 996)

$1,200-$1,400

"Escargot"
in amber glass, circa
1920, 8 5/8" tall. (M p.
424, No. 931)

$10,000+

"Espalion"
in iridescent blue
glass, circa 1927, 7
1/8" tall. (M p. 438,
No. 996)

$3,000+

Vases

"Esterel"
circa 1923, in cased
opalescent glass with
blue patina, engraved
R Lalique France No.
941, 6" tall. (M p. 426,
No. 941)
$1,600+

"Feuilles"
in opalescent glass,
circa 1934, 7 1/8"
tall. (M p. 460, No.
10-880)
$1,800+

"Esterel"
in clear and frosted
glass with blue-green
patina, engraved R.
Lalique, 6" tall. (M p.
426, No. 941)
$1,100-$1,400

"Fontainebleau"
circa 1930, in deep blue glass with grayish patina, engraved R. Lalique France
No. 1011, 6 7/8" tall. (M p. 446, No. 10-36)
$5,500-$6,000

"Esterel"
circa 1923, in deep
amber glass, molded R
LALIQUE, 6" tall. (M
p. 426, No. 941)
$1,800-$2,000

"Font-Romeau"
circa 1936, in clear
and frosted glass,
stenciled R. LALIQUE
FRANCE, 8 5/8" tall.
(M p. 463, No. 10-
893)
$1,500-$1,700

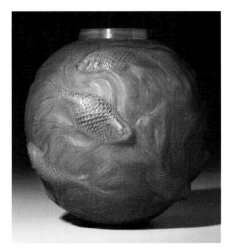

"Formose"
circa 1924, in cased gray glass, molded R.
LALIQUE, 7 1/8" tall. (M p. 425, No. 934)
$4,000-$4,500

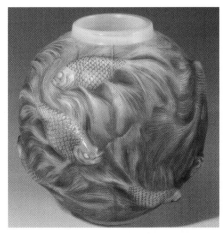

"Formose"
circa 1924, in cased opalescent glass with blue
patina, stenciled R. LALIQUE FRANCE, 6 1/2" tall.
(M p. 425, No. 934)
$2,200-$2,400

"Formose"
in cased opalescent glass with gray patina, molded
R. LALIQUE, 6 1/2" tall. (Ref. M p. 425, No. 934)
$2,700-$3,000

"Formose"
circa 1924, in cased
opalescent yellow
glass with sepia
patina, molded R.
LALIQUE, 6 1/2" tall.
(M p. 425, No. 934)

$3,000-$3,500

"Formose"
circa 1924, in emerald
green glass, engraved
R. Lalique France, 7
1/8" tall. (M p. 425,
No. 934)
$4,000-$5,000

"Formose"
circa 1924, in white
opalescent glass with
sepia patina, engraved
R. Lalique France, 7
1/8" tall. (M p. 425,
No. 934)

$2,400-$2,600

"Formose"
in cased red glass
with traces of white
patina, circa 1924, 7
1/8" tall. (M p. 425,
No. 934)

$5,000+

Vases

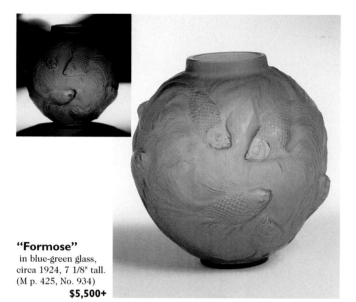

"Formose"
in blue-green glass,
circa 1924, 7 1/8" tall.
(M p. 425, No. 934)
$5,500+

"Formose"
in emerald green
glass, circa 1924, 7
1/8" tall. (M p. 425,
No. 934)
$8,000+

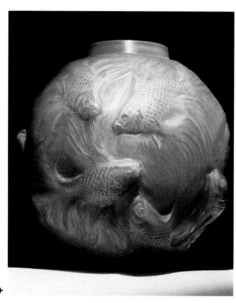

"Formose"
circa 1924, in cased
lavender-gray glass,
engraved R. Lalique
France, 6 3/4" tall. (M
p. 425, No. 934)
$12,000+

"Formose"
in golden amber glass,
circa 1924, 7 1/8" tall.
(M p. 425, No. 934)
$4,500+

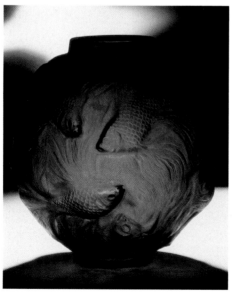

"Formose"
in topaz glass, circa
1924, 7 1/8" tall. (M p.
425, No. 934)
$3,500+

"Formose"
circa 1924, in cased
red and amber glass
with traces of white
patina, engraved R.
Lalique France, 6 3/4"
tall. (M p. 425, No.
934)
$7,000+

"Formose"
circa 1924, in red glass with traces of white patina, molded R. Lalique, 6 3/4"
tall. (M p. 425, No. 934)

$5,000+

"Fougeres"
in blue-green glass, circa 1912, 7 1/1/2" tall. (M p. 422, No. 923)

$5,000+

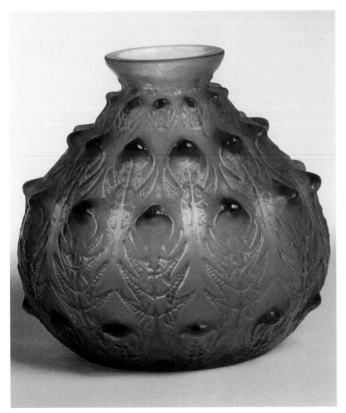

"Fougeres"
in charcoal gray glass, circa 1912, 7 1/1/2" tall. (M p. 422, No. 923)

$4,000+

"Fougeres"
in blue glass, circa 1912, 7 1/1/2" tall. (M p. 422, No. 923)

$7,500+

Vases

"Gobelet Six Figurines"
circa 1912, in topaz glass, wheel-cut R. LALIQUE, 7 7/8" tall. (M p. 417, No. 903)

$2,200-$2,400

"Graines"
in pale red glass, circa 1930, 7 7/8" tall. (M p. 447, No. 1042)

$4,000+

"Grande Boule Lierre"
circa 1920, in satin glass with green and brown patina, 14 1/4" tall. (M p. 410, No. 877)

$30,000+

"Grenade"
in cased red glass,
circa 1930, 4 3/4" tall.
(M p. 448, No. 1045)
$5,000+

"Grenade"
circa 1930, in black
glass, stenciled R.
LALIQUE, engraved
France, 4 3/4" tall. (M
p. 448, No. 10-45)
$2,300-$2,500

"Grenade"
circa 1930, in black
glass with white
patina, stenciled R.
LALIQUE, 4 3/4" tall.
(M p. 448, No. 1045)
$2,000-$2,500

"Grenade"
in deep amber glass,
engraved R. Lalique
France, 4 3/4" tall.
(Ref. M p. 448, No.
10-45)
$2,800-$3,200

"Grenade"
circa 1930, in deep
amber glass, engraved
R. Lalique France, 4"
tall. (M p. 448, No.
10-45)
$1,500-$1,700

"Grenade"
circa 1930, in
sapphire blue glass,
stenciled R. LALIQUE,
4 3/4" tall. (M p. 448,
No. 10-45)
$2,200-$2,400

Vases

"Grimpereaux"
in deep topaz glass, wheel-cut R. LALIQUE. (Ref. M p. 436, No. 987)

$2,000-$2,500

"Gros Scarabees"
in deep amber glass with white patina, stenciled R. LALIQUE FRANCE. (M p. 415, No. 892.)

$15,000-$18,000

"Gros Scarabees"
circa 1923, in cased jade green glass with white patina, stenciled R. LALIQUE FRANCE, 11 5/8" tall. (M p. 415, No. 892)

$30,000+

"Lievres"
in clear and frosted glass with blue-gray patina, molded R. LALIQUE. (M p. 426, No. 982.)

$1,500-$1,800

"Gui"
in cobalt blue glass
with white patina,
circa 1920, 6 3/4" tall.
(M p. 427, No. 948)
$4,500+

"Gui"
circa 1920, in cased
opalescent glass with
blue patina, molded R.
LALIQUE, engraved
Lalique, 6 3/4" tall. (M
p. 427, No. 948)
$1,800+

"Gui"
circa 1920, in
opalescent glass,
molded R.LALIQUE
and engraved R.
Lalique France, 6 3/4"
tall. (Ref. M p. 427,
No. 948)
$700-$800

"Gui"
circa 1920, in
opalescent glass with
gray patina, molded R.
LALIQUE, 6 3/4" tall.
(M p. 427, No. 948)
$600-$700

"Gui"
circa 1920, in white
opalescent glass with
green patina, molded
R. LALIQUE, 6 3/4"
tall. (M p. 427, No.
948)
$750-$850

Vases

"Guirlandes"
in clear and frosted glass with black enamel decoration, circa 1935, 8 1/4 in. tall. (M p. 462, No. 10-887)

$3,000+

"Hirondelles"
in opalescent glass with gray patina, circa 1919, 9 1/4" tall. (M p. 414, No. 889)

$3,500+

"Hirondelles"
in cherry red glass with white patina, circa 1919, 9 1/4" tall. (M p. 414, No. 889)

$5,000+

"Honfleur"
circa 1926, in clear and frosted glass, wheel-cut R. LALIQUE FRANCE, engraved No. 994, 5 1/2" tall. (M p. 437, No. 994)

$900-$1,000

"Ibis"
in olive green glass with white patina, circa 1934,
9 1/1/2" tall. (M p. 459, No. 1099)

$3,500+

"Inseparables"
in clear and frosted glass with blue patina, circa
1919, 13 3/8" tall. (M p. 414, No. 887)

$12,000+

"Koudour"
circa 1926, in clear glass with black enamel
decoration, molded R. LALIQUE, engraved R.
Lalique France, 7 1/8" long. (M p. 432, No. 968)

$6,000-$7,000

"Lagamar"
circa 1926, in clear and frosted glass with black enamel decoration, wheel-cut
R. LALIQUE, 7 1/4" tall. (M p. 432, No. 967)

$9,000-$12,000

"Laiterons"
in amber glass with gray patina, circa 1931, 3 1/4" tall. (M p. 454, No. 1072)

$1,200+

Vases

"Languedoc"
circa 1932, in clear and frosted glass with sepia patina, engraved R. Lalique France, 8 3/4" tall. (M p. 443 No. 1041)

$5,500-$6,200

"Languedoc"
circa 1932, in cased green glass with white patina, engraved R. Lalique France, 8 3/4" tall. (M p. 443, No. 1041)

$30,000+

"Laurier"
circa 1922, in amber satin glass, molded R. LALIQUE, 7 1/2" tall. (M p. 427, No. 947)

$2,000+

"Laurier"
circa 1922, in opalescent glass, wheel-cut R. LALIQUE FRANCE, engraved 947, 7" tall. (M p. 427, No. 947)

$1,200-$1,500

"Le Mans"
in blue-green glass, circa 1931, 4" tall. (M p. 454, No. 1074)

$4,000+

"Lezard et Bluets"
circa 1920, in opaque black glass with traces of white patina, with sharp mold and wide neck ring, wheel-cut R. LALIQUE with long L, 13 3/8" tall. (M p. 410, No. 879)

$8,000+

"Le Mans"
circa 1931, in amber glass with white patina, stenciled R. LALIQUE FRANCE, 4 1/8" tall. (M p. 454, No. 1074)

$1,800-$2,200

Vases

"Malesherbes"
circa 1927, in clear
and frosted glass with
traces of sepia patina,
engraved R. Lalique
France no 1014, 9
1/8" tall. (M p. 442,
No. 1014)

$1,300-$1,500

"Malines"
circa 1924, in clear
and frosted glass with
gray patina, engraved
R. Lalique France, 5
1/8" tall. (M p. 429,
No. 957)

$350-$400

"Malesherbes"
circa 1927, in deep
amber glass with
white patina, engraved
R. Lalique France No.
1014, 9 1/8" tall. (M p.
442, No. 1014)

$2,600-$3,000

"Malesherbes"
circa 1928, in
opalescent glass with
gray patina, stenciled
R. LALIQUE, 9 1/8"
tall. (M p. 432, No.
10-14)

$1,400-$1,600

"Malines"
circa 1924, in blue glass,
stenciled R. LALIQUE,
engraved France, 5 1/8" tall. (M
p. 429, No. 957)

$2,000+

"Marisa"
in clear and frosted glass, circa 1927, 9 1/1/2" tall.
(M p. 439, No. 1002)

$5,000+

"Martinets"
circa 1970, in clear and frosted glass, engraved
Lalique France, 9 1/2" tall.

$700-$800

"Meandres"
in opalescent glass, circa 1934, 6 1/1/2" tall. (M p.
459, No. 10-876)

$1,800+

"Meduse"
in teal green glass,
circa 1921, 6 7/8" tall.
(M p. 428, No. 950)

$6,000+

"Mesanges"
circa 1931, in clear
and frosted glass,
stenciled R. LALIQUE
FRANCE, 13" tall. (M
p. 452, No. 10-64)

$2,800-$3,200

"Meudon"
circa 1933, in clear
glass, stenciled R.
LALIQUE France,
5" tall, together with
a footed vase, circa
1960, in clear and
frosted glass, 6" tall.
(M p. 460, No. 10-878)

$500-$600/pair

"Milan"
in blue glass with
white patina, circa
1929, 11 1/4" tall. (M
p. 444, No. 1025)

$20,000+

Vases

"Moissac"
in electric blue glass, without foot, circa
1927, 5 1/8" tall. (M p. 437, No. 992)
$4,000+

"Moissac"
in opalescent glass, without foot, circa 1927, 5 1/8" tall. (M p. 437, No. 992)
$2,800+

"Moissac"
circa 1950, in opalescent glass, footed version, stenciled LALIQUE FRANCE, 5
1/2" tall. (M p. 437, No. 992)
$600-$700

"Moissac"
in deep topaz glass,
molded R. LALIQUE,
5 1/2" tall. (Ref. M p.
437, No. 992)

$2,000-$2,300

"Moissac"
circa 1927, in topaz
glass, wheel-cut R
LALIQUE FRANCE,
5 1/2" tall. (M p. 437,
No. 992)

$1,600-$1,800

"Moissac"
circa 1927, in yellow
glass, wheel-cut R
LALIQUE FRANCE,
5 1/8" tall. (M p. 437,
No. 992)

$1,500-$1,700

"Moissac"
in yellow amber glass,
wheel-cut R. Lalique
France, 5 1/8" tall. (M
p. 437, No. 992)

$1,700-$2,000

"Monnaie du Pape"
in deep amber glass, circa 1914, 9" tall. (M p. 416,
No. 897)

$6,000+

"Morgan"
in clear glass with black enamel decoration, circa
1926, 6 1/4" tall. (M p. 432, No. 969)

$2,000+

"Myrrhis"
circa 1926, in topaz glass, molded R. LALIQUE
FRANCE, 7 1/2" tall. (M p. 435, No. 983)

$1,400-$1,500

Vases

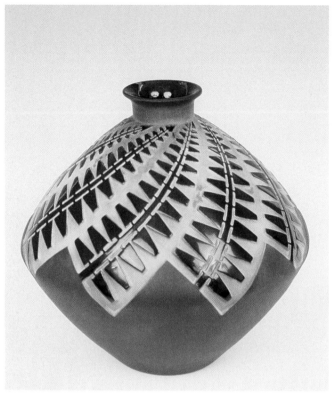

"Montargis"
circa 1930, in opaque black glass with white patina, wheel-cut R. Lalique and the style number, 1022. (M p. 443, No. 1022)

$1,500

"Montargis"
a vase which was originally clear and frosted but which has been irradiated to change the color to a deep purple. The irradiation affects the value negatively.

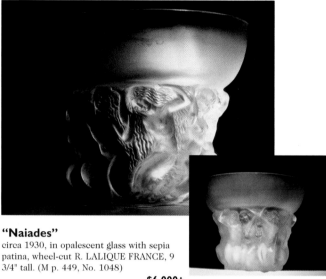

"Naiades"
circa 1930, in opalescent glass with sepia patina, wheel-cut R. LALIQUE FRANCE, 9 3/4" tall. (M p. 449, No. 1048)

$6,000+

"Nefliers"
circa 1923, in clear and frosted glass with blue patina, engraved R. Lalique France no. 940, 5 1/2" tall. (M p. 426, No. 940)

$800-$900

"Nefliers" and "Domremy"
two vases, in clear and frosted glass with sepia patina, and cased opalescent glass. Engraved R. Lalique France and stenciled R. LALIQUE FRANCE. "Domremy" with internal cracks to base. (M pp. 424 and 434, Nos. 940 and 979)

$400-$500/pair

"Nimroud"
in clear glass with black enamel decoration, circa 1926, 7 3/4 in. tall. (M p. 432, No. 970)

$3,000+

"Oleron"
circa 1927, in cased opalescent glass with green patina, engraved R. Lalique France No. 1008. (M p. 440, No. 1008), 3 1/2" tall.

$2,500+

"Oleron"
circa 1927, in clear and frosted glass with traces of sepia patina, engraved R. Lalique France. (M p. 440, No. 1008), 3 1/2" tall.

$800-$1,000

"Ondines"
modern, in clear and frosted glass, engraved Lalique France, 9 1/8" tall.

$700-$800

Vases

"Oranges"
circa 1926, in clear and frosted glass with brown enamel decoration, molded R. LALIQUE, 11 1/1/2" tall. (M p. 431, No. 964)

$30,000+

"Oran"
in opalescent glass, circa 1927, 10 1/4" tall. (M p. 439, No. 999)

$20,000+

"Orly"
circa 1935, in clear glass, stenciled R. LALIQUE FRANCE, 5 1/2" tall. (M p. 462, No. 10-891)

$1,700-$1,900

"Ormeaux"
circa 1926, in cased
opalescent glass,
engraved R. Lalique
France no 984, 6 1/2"
tall. (M p. 435, No.
984)

$1,000-$1,200

"Ormeaux"
in charcoal gray
glass vase with white
patina, engraved R.
Lalique France No.
984, 6 1/2" tall. (Ref.
M p. 435, No. 984)

$3,000-$3,500

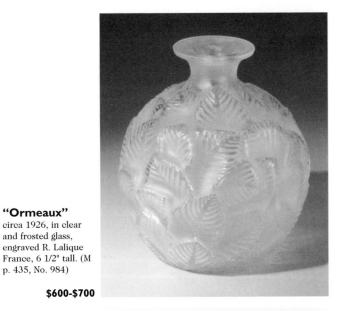

"Ormeaux"
circa 1926, in clear
and frosted glass,
engraved R. Lalique
France, 6 1/2" tall. (M
p. 435, No. 984)

$600-$700

"Ormeaux"
circa 1926, in clear
and frosted glass with
green patina, engraved
R. Lalique France no
984, 6 1/2" tall. (M p.
435, No. 984)

$750-$850

"Ormeaux"
circa 1926, in
opalescent glass,
engraved R. Lalique
France, 6 1/2" tall. (M
p. 435, No. 984)

$450-$500

"Ormeaux"
in cased blue-green
glass, circa 1926, 6
5/8" tall. (M p. 435,
No. 984)

$3,500+

Vases

"Ornis"
circa 1926, in clear and frosted glass with gray patina, wheel-cut R. LALIQUE FRANCE, 8 1/2" tall. (M p. 434, No. 976)

$1,600-$1,700

"Ornis"
circa 1926, in opalescent glass, wheel-cut R. LALIQUE FRANCE, 8 5/8" tall. (M p. 434, No. 976)

$5,500-$6,500

"Ornis"
circa 1926, in topaz glass, wheel-cut R. LALIQUE FRANCE, 8 5/8" tall. (M p. 434, No. 976)

$1,800-$2,200

"Oursin"
circa 1935, in clear and frosted glass, stenciled R. LALIQUE, 7 1/4" tall. (M p. 442, No. 10-888)

$1,700-$1,800

"Oursin"
circa 1935, in clear and frosted glass with white patina, stenciled R. LALIQUE, engraved France, 7 1/8" tall. (M p. 462, No. 10-888)

$1,200-$1,400

"Palissy"
circa 1926, in cased opalescent glass, engraved R. Lalique France, 6 1/3" tall.
(M p. 434, No. 980)

$1,700-$2,000

"Palissy"
circa 1926, in opalescent glass with blue patina, engraved R Lalique France no 980, 6 1/3" tall. (M p. 434, No. 980)

$1,000-$1,200

"Pan"
circa 1937, in clear and frosted glass with gray patina, stenciled R. LALIQUE FRANCE, 12 1/2" long. (M p. 465, No. 10-904)

$5,500-$6,000

Vases

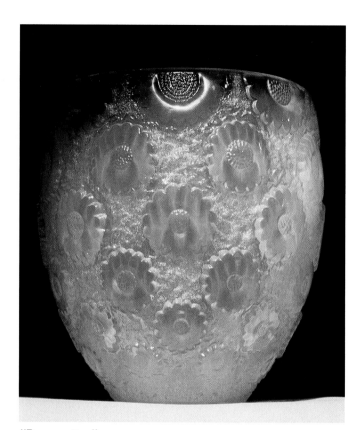

"Pan"
circa 1950, in clear and frosted glass with sepia patina, stenciled LALIQUE FRANCE, 12 1/2" long.

$4,500-$5,000

"Paquerettes"
in opalescent glass, circa 1934, 7 1/4" tall. (M p. 460, No. 10-877)

$1,800+

"Penthivere"
circa 1926, in topaz glass with grayish patina, engraved R. Lalique France No. 1011, 10 1/4" tall. (M p. 441, No. 10-11)

$10,000-$12,000

"Penthivere"
circa 1926, in cobalt blue glass with white patina, engraved R. LALIQUE, 10 1/4" tall. (M p. 441, No. 1011)

$15,000+

"Perles"
circa 1925, in opalescent glass, molded R. LALIQUE, 4 3/4" tall. (M p. 430, No. 959)

$800-$1,000

"Perigord"
circa 1928, in opalescent glass, engraved R. Lalique France, 6" diameter. (M p. 438, No. 9003)

$1,800-$2,000

"Perles"
in cased gray satin glass, circa 1925, molded R. LALIQUE, 4 3/4" tall. (M p. 430, No. 959)

$2,000+

"Picardie"
in opalescent glass, circa 1927, 9 1/1/2" tall. (M p. 440, No. 1006)

$3,500+

Vases

"Perruches"
circa 1919, in cased opalescent glass with blue patina, molded R. LALIQUE, 10" tall. (M p. 410, No. 876)

$6,000-$7,000

"Plumes"
circa 1920, in cased opalescent glass, engraved Lalique, molded R. LALIQUE, 8 1/4" tall. (M p. 427, No. 944)

$1,000-$1,200

"Perruches"
circa 1919, in clear and frosted glass, molded R. LALIQUE, 9 1/2" tall. (M p. 410, No. 876)

$2,800-$3,200

"Plumes"
circa 1920, in clear and frosted glass, molded R. LALIQUE, 8 1/4" tall. (M p. 427, No. 944)

$550-$650

"Perruches"
in deep green glass, molded R. LALIQUE, 9 1/2" tall. (Ref. M p. 410, No. 876)

$16,000-$18,000

"Plumes"
circa 1920, in opalescent glass, molded R. LALIQUE, engraved France, 8 1/4" tall. (M p. 427, No. 944)

$600-$700

"Piriac"
circa 1930, in blue glass, stenciled R. LALIQUE FRANCE, 7 1/4" tall. (M p. 447, No. 1043)

$4,200-$4,800

"Piriac"
a LALIQUE vase, circa 1930, in deep topaz glass, wheel-cut R. LALIQUE FRANCE, 7 1/4" tall. (M p. 447, No. 1043)

$4,200-$4,800

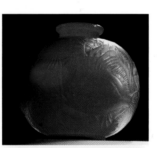

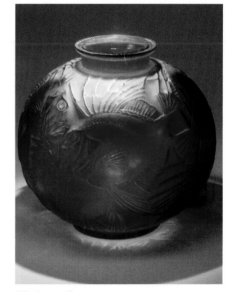

"Poissons"
in red glass with a gold tinge and white patina, circa 1921, molded R. Lalique, 9 3/8" tall. (M p. 422, No. 925)

$18,000+

"Poissons"
circa 1921, in cased red glass, engraved Lalique, molded R. LALIQUE, 9" tall. (M p. 422, No. 925)

$15,000-$17,000

Vases

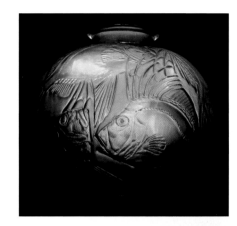

"Poissons"
in emerald green glass, circa 1921, molded R. Lalique, 9 3/8" tall. (M p. 422, No. 925)

$12,000+

"Poissons"
in blue glass, circa 1921, molded R. Lalique, 9 3/8" tall. (M p. 422, No. 925)

$10,000+

"Poissons"
circa 1921, in cased opalescent glass, engraved R. Lalique France No. 925, 9 5/8" tall, neck slightly polished. (M p. 422, No. 925)

$2,500-$3,000

"Poissons"
in cased teal green glass, circa 1921, molded R. Lalique, 9 3/8" tall. (M p. 422, No. 925)

$15,000+

"Poissons"
circa 1922, in cased turquoise glass, molded R. Lalique, 9 3/8" tall. (M p. 422, No. 925)

$18,000+

"Quatre Panneaux"
circa 1928, in clear and frosted glass with sepia patina, stenciled R. LALIQUE FRANCE, 7 1/4" tall. (M p. 468, No. 10-920)

$1,400-$1,500

"Raisins"
circa 1928, in clear and frosted glass with blue patina, wheel-cut R. LALIQUE FRANCE, 6 1/4" tall. (M p. 448, No. 1032)

$550-$650

Vases

"Rampillon"
in opalescent glass, molded R. LALIQUE. (M p. 437, No. 991.)

$1,000-$1,200

"Rampillon"
circa 1927, in opalescent glass with blue-gray patina, wheel-cut R. LALIQUE FRANCE, 5" tall. (M p. 437, No. 991)

$1,000-$1,200

"Rampillon"
circa 1927, in topaz glass, wheel-cut R. LALIQUE FRANCE, 5" tall. (M p. 437, No. 991)

$1,100-$1,500

"Rampillon"
in yellow amber glass, wheel-cut R. Lalique France, 5" tall. (M p. 437, No. 991)

$1,700-$2,000

"Rampillon"
circa 1927, in yellow glass, stenciled R. LALIQUE FRANCE, 5" tall. (M p. 437, No. 991)

$1,200-$1,400

"Ronces"
in cased opalescent glass with blue gray patina, molded R. LALIQUE, 9 1/2" tall. (M p. 427, No. 946)

$2,800-$3,200

"Salmonides"
in cased lavender glass, circa 1928, 11 3/8" tall. (M p. 442, No. 1015)

$7,000+

"Ronces"
circa 1921, in cased yellow glass, molded R. LALIQUE, engraved Lalique, 9 1/2" tall. (M p. 427, No. 946)

$4,800-$5,400

"Salmonides"
in clear and frosted glass, circa 1928, 11 3/8" tall. (M p. 442, No. 1015)

$3,500+

Vases

Two modern vases
including "Rosine" and another vase with a bird design. Both engraved Lalique France, taller 4 7/8".

$225-$275/pair

"Sauge"
in clear and frosted glass, molded R. LALIQUE FRANCE. (M p. 425, No. 925)

$1,800-$2,000

"Sauterelles"
circa 1912, in clear and frosted glass with traces of blue and green patina, engraved R. Lalique, 10 1/2" tall. (M p. 414, No. 888)

$4,000-$5,000

"Sauterelles"
in frosted glass with green and blue patina, engraved R. Lalique, 10 1/2" tall. (Ref. M p. 414, No. 888)

$5,000-$5,800

"St. Emilion"
a vase or wine cooler,
circa 1942, in clear and
frosted glass, engraved
R. Lalique France, 10"
tall. (M p. 472, No. 10-
939)

$1,200-$1,500

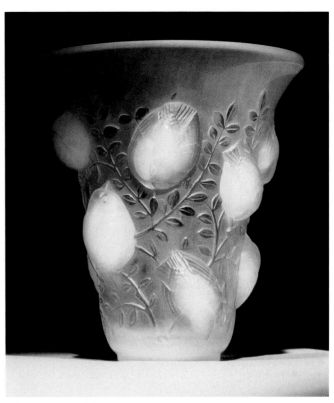

"Saint Tropez"
circa 1937, in opalescent
glass, stenciled R.
LALIQUE FRANCE, 7 1/2"
tall. (M p. 467, No. 10-
915)

$1,200-$1,400

"Saint-Francois"
circa 1930, in cased opalescent glass with blue patina, stenciled R. LALIQUE
FRANCE, 6 7/8". (M p. 450, No. 1055)

$2,400-$2,800

"Sauge"
in blue-green glass with white
patina, circa 1923, 10 1/4" tall. (M
p. 425, No. 935)

$2,000+

"Saint-Francois"
circa 1930, in clear opalescent glass, stenciled R. LALIQUE FRANCE, 7" tall. (M
p. 450, No. 1055)

$1,900-$2,100

"Sauterelles"
in blue glass, circa 1912, engraved R. Lalique, 11" tall. (M p. 414, No. 888)
$9,500+

"Serpent"
in purple glass, circa 1924, 10 1/4" tall. (M p. 416, No. 896)
$40,000

"Sauterelles"
in electric blue glass, circa 1912, engraved R. Lalique, 11" tall. (M p. 414, No. 888)
$12,000+

"Sauterelles"
circa 1912, in clear and frosted glass with strong blue and green patina, engraved R. Lalique France, 10 1/2" tall. (M p. 414, No. 888)
$6,000-$7,000

"Sirenes Avec Bouchon Figurine"
in opalescent glass, with stopper, circa 1920, 14 1/1/2" tall with stopper. (M p. 411, No. 883)
$7,000+

"Six Figurines"
in clear and frosted glass with sepia patina, wheel-cut R. LALIQUE. (M p. 414, No. 886.)

$4,500-$5,000

"Six Figurines et Masques"
circa 1912, in opalescent glass with blue patina, engraved R. Lalique France No. 886, 9 7/8" tall. (M p. 414, No. 886)

$6,000-$6,500

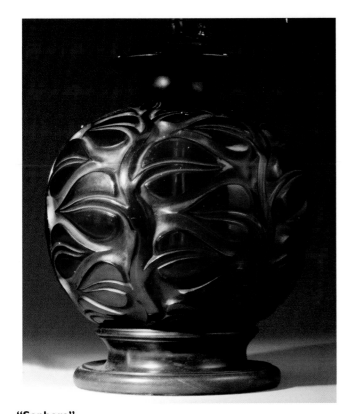

"Sophora"
circa 1926, in deep amber glass, vase 10 1/4" tall, now drilled and mounted as an electric table lamp. Marks not visible. (M p. 434, No. 977)

$1,100-$1,300

"Spirales"
in opalescent glass, circa 1930, 6 1/1/2" tall. (M p. 451, No. 1060)

$3,000+

Vases

"Sylvie"
modern, in clear and frosted glass with original flower frog, Engraved Lalique France, 8 1/4" tall.

$325-$375

"Tortues"
circa 1926, in cased butterscotch glass, molded R. LALIQUE, 10 3/4" tall. (M p. 432, No. 966)

$40,000+

"Tourbillons"
circa 1926, in clear glass with black enameled highlights, wheel-cut R. LALIQUE, 8" tall. (M p. 433, No. 973)

$40,000-$42,000

"Tourbillons"
circa 1926, in clear glass with black enameled highlights, wheel-cut R. LALIQUE, 7 7/8" tall. (M p. 433, No. 973)

$45,000+

"Tournesol"
circa 1927, in clear and frosted glass with yellow patina, engraved R. Lalique France, 4 3/4" tall. (M p. 440, No. 1007)

$1,100-$1,300

"Tulipes"
circa 1930, in opalescent glass, engraved R. Lalique France, 7 1/4" tall. (M p. 449, No. 1049)

$2,500-$3,000

"Violettes"
circa 1921, in clear and frosted glass with blue patina, engraved R. Lalique, 6 1/4" tall. (M p. 424, No. 930)

$1,200-$1,400

"Volutes"
circa 1926, in gray/brown glass with acid-etched decoration, designed by Suzanne Lalique, 16 1/2" tall. (M p. 413, No. 885/J)

No established value

Other Lalique Items

This section includes annual plates, candlesticks, clocks, desk items, medallions, and rocker blotters.

Four limited-edition annual plates
1972, 1973, 1974, and 1975, engraved Lalique France, each 8 1/2" diameter.
$300-$350/set

"Entrelacs"
cabinet/armoire, 1935, 74 7/8" tall. (M p. 891, Nos. 29A and 29B)
No established value

"Raisins"
a tall goblet, amber glass and silver, circa 1902, 6" tall. (M p. 804, C)
$28,000+

Chalice
with pine cone motif, silver and opalescent glass, circa 1904, marked No. 2 from a series of 50, 7 1/2" tall.
$35,000-$40,000

Other Lalique Items

"Auriac"
a candelabrum, designed circa 1944, this example 1960, in clear and frosted glass, 9 1/8" long, together with a modern Lalique ashtray, "Caravelle." Both engraved Lalique France.

$200-$250/pair

"Inseparables"
a clock, circa 1926, in opalescent glass, fitted into an Art Deco blue and white hard-stone mount of the period, molded R. LALIQUE, 4" tall. (M p. 377, No. 765)

$1,500-$2,000

"Soudan"
a pair of candlesticks, circa 1934, in clear and frosted glass, stenciled R. LALIQUE FRANCE, 2" tall. (Ref. M p. 611, No. 2124)

$1,200-$1,500

"Inseparables"
a clock frame, circa 1926, in clear and frosted glass, molded R. LALIQUE, 4 1/3" tall. (M p. 377, No. 765)

$600-$700

An early cane handle
circa 1905, in clear and frosted glass with sepia patina, 3 3/4" long. (M p. 141)

$600-$700

"Perles"
dressing table garniture.

$1,000-$1,200/set

"Moineaux"
a clock for ATO, circa 1924, in clear and frosted glass with sepia patina, original Art Deco face and modern quartz movement, molded R. LALIQUE, 6 1/8" tall. (M p. 369, No. B)

$4,500-$5,000

"Garnitures de Toilette Epines"
a seven-piece dressing table set, in clear and frosted glass with gray patina, with all four sizes of perfume bottle, large and small covered boxes, and pin tray. Each piece with molded signature. (Ref. M p. 344)

$2,500-$3,000/set

"Acanthes"
a jardiniere, circa 1927, in clear and frosted glass with sepia patina, wheel-cut R. LALIQUE FRANCE, engraved No. 3460, 18" long. (M p. 773, No. 3460)

$900-$1,000

"Cigalia"
a pot de creme for Roger et Gallet, circa 1924, in clear and frosted glass with green patina, 3 3/4" tall. (M p. 970, No. 1)

$750-$850

"Deux Sirenes Couche Face en Face"
a rocker blotter, circa 1920, in clear and frosted glass with gray patina, original metal, molded R. LALIQUE, engraved France, 6 1/3" long. (M p. 245, No. 157)

$2,000-$2,400

"Faune et Nymphe"
a rocker blotter, circa 1920, in clear and frosted glass with sepia patina, original metal, molded R. LALIQUE, engraved France, 6 1/3" long. (M p. 245, No. 153)

$1,600-$1,900

"Feuilles D'Artichaut"
a rocker blotter, circa 1920, in clear and frosted glass with sepia patina, original metal, molded R. LALIQUE, 6 1/3" long. (M p. 245, No. 155)

$1,200-$1,400

A rare souvenir program
for the Journee de Sarah Bernhardt with cover illustration by Rene Lalique, circa 1893. Folio: 33" by 24 1/21/2" includes illustrations by Georges Clairin and Rene Foy, and features cover illustrations by Lalique depicting Sarah Bernhardt as "Theodora" and illustrations of Lalique's commemorative medallion made for the event.

$2,400-$2,800

Fakes and Reproductions

By Mark Chervenka

From Antique Trader Guide to Fakes and Reproductions

There are several considerations when evaluating Lalique. There are genuine Lalique pieces made after 1945 with forged pre-1945 marks; new glass (especially from the Czech Republic) with forged marks that copy Lalique patterns; and pre-1945 glass by other manufacturers with forged Lalique marks.

Virtually all authentic Lalique glass is marked. Pieces made before René Lalique's death in 1945 were marked "R.Lalique," usually followed by the word "France." After 1945, the "R" was dropped and the mark was simply "Lalique, France." The single letter R is commonly forged on current Lalique to suggest a piece was made before 1945. Pre-1945 clear Lalique fluoresces a soft yellow-green to yellow under long-wave black light. Clear Lalique made after 1945 does not fluoresce. Since 1980, Lalique engraved marks have also included the ® symbol, which was never used before 1980. If the initial "R" appeared with that symbol, it would automatically be a forgery.

New Art Deco-styled glass made today in the Czech Republic is frequently sold as "unmarked" Lalique or sold with forged Lalique marks. Most is inferior in quality to Lalique. One quick test of quality is to look for mold seams. Mold seams are almost impossible to find in genuine Lalique. Seams on the inexpensive copycat pieces are usually very obvious. Most original Lalique has at least some polishing, either on the base or top rim. The look-alike pieces are generally frosted all over.

Glass from other manufacturers made before 1945 seldom passes the quality tests described above. Forged marks on Lalique imitations made before 1945 have the same general problems as the other typical forgeries.

Most Lalique was pressed and therefore does not have a pontil. Glass is uniformly high quality without flaws.

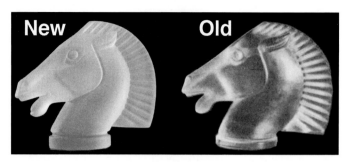

New frosted clear glass horse head made today in Czech Republic, left. Original, circa 1929, Lalique "Longchamps" hood ornament, right. Czech piece has been in the market since the early 1990s. There are also new Czech copies of other Lalique hood ornaments including Lalique's Victoire and Vitesse. The new piece is gray and chalky, with obvious mold seams.

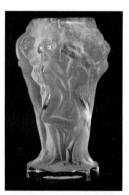

New frosted glass 17" lamp, left, with molded mark, "Made in France." New 5" frosted glass vase with nudes, right, made today in Czech Republic, no mark. These and other similar new pieces are frequently found with forged Lalique marks.

New copycat frosted glass perfume bottle made in Taiwan. Frequently seen with forged marks. Stopper made with double flower.

Original Deaux Fleurs Lalique perfume marked "R. Lalique." Re-issued after 1945 without "R." Original stopper is a single flower.

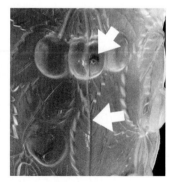

New circa 1990s 7" Czech frosted glass vase with cherries, right, made from original 1930s mold. New production has obvious mold seams (left) and unmelted impurities in glass.

Lalique marks have included the registered symbol, an R in a circle ® since 1980. This symbol is virtually unknown in pre-1945 Lalique marks.

Obvious mold seams on most new Czech pieces continue down body on to the bottom rim.

French-to-English

Lalique borrowed heavily from plants, animals, and French locations when naming the myriad of exquisite glassware, from perfume bottles to vases, that were produced over the years. Eagles, trees, deer, flowers, and squirrels were among mother nature's contribution to Lalique labels. French cities and regions ranged from Alicante to Vezelay. The human, emotional, and mythological names included love, victory, angel, dancer, and mermaid.

Here is a selected list of French words used to describe or label Lalique pieces and their English translations:

Acacia: Locust tree
Actinia: Sea anemone
Aigle: Eagle
Aigrettes: Bird crests or plumes
Alicante: A Spanish city on the Mediterranean
Ambre: Amber
Amelie: Amelia
Amies: Friends
Amour: Love
Amphitrite: Mythical goddess of the sea and wife of Poseidon
Anemones: Colorful sea animals
Ange et Colombe: Angel and dove
Antilope: Antelope
Archers: Same in English
Au Coeur des Calices: A brand of perfume
Auriac: A French village, Brue Auriac
Avalon: An ancient British isle
Bacchantes: Mythological Greek women
Bague Feuilles: Ring of paper
Bagatelle: Trifles
Baies: Bays or berries
Barrette Oiseaux: A glass and metal bar pin (oiseaux is French for birds)
Beliers: Rams
Bellecour: Beautiful courtyard
Belle Saison: Beautiful season
Biches: Hinds or does
Bluets: Perennial cornflowers with tiny blue flowers
Bordure Epines: Border of thorn bushes
Borrome: An Italian island
Bouchardon: A French sculptor in the 18th century
La Bresse: A French mountain village
Bulbes: Bulbs
Calendal: A 19th century novel set in Provenza
Calypso: Music or muse
Camaret: A village in Brittany
Camargue: A province in southern France
Camille: A woman's name; Camille Claudel was a well-known late 19th century artist
Canard: Duck
Caravelle: Ship
Cerises: Cherries
Cernay: A city in France
Chamois: A leather cloth
Chamonix: An Alps area
Chardons: Thistles
Chataignier: Chestnut tree
Chat Assis: Sitting cat
Chat Couche: Crouching cat
Chevre: Goat
Chien: Dog
Chrysis: A backward leaning nude figure C ised in Europe, originally from India
Coq Houdan: A breed of French chicken
Coq Nain: Another breed of chicken
Coquilles: Shells

Copellia: A classical ballet
Croisiere: Cruise
Croix aux Quatre Anges: Cross of Four Angels
Courges: Gourds
Cytise: Ebony tree
Dahlias: A type of flower
Daim: Buck or male deer
Danseuse: Dancer or ballerina
Dans La Nuit: In the night
Dauphins: Dolphins, also sons of kings
Davos: A Swiss mountain resort
Degas: An artist of the late 19th century
Deux Sirenes Couche Face en Face: Two women crouching face to face
Dentele: Jagged or scalloped
Dindon: Turkey
Domremy: Joan of Arc's hometown
Dordogne: A French region
Druides: Members of an ancient religion
Ecailles: Oyster shells
Ecureuil: Squirrel
Eglantines: Wild rose flowers
Enfants: Infants or Babies
Entrelacs: Intertwined or interlaced
Epernay: Capital city of Champagne
Epicea: Spruce
Epines: Thorns
Escargot: Snail
Espalion: A region of the Pyrenees
Esterel: A city in southern France on the Riviera
Faucon: Falcon
Faune et Nymphe: Wildlife and nymph
Fauvettes: Warblers
Femmes dans les Fleurs
Feuilles: Leaves
Feuilles D'Artichaut: Artichoke leaves
Feuilles De Lierre: Ivy leaves
Fille d'Eve: A brand of perfume for Nina Ricci
Flacons: Flasks
Fleur: Flower
Fleurons: Flowrets
Floride: Florida
Fronton Panier de Fleur: Basket of flowers
Fontainebleau: A famous French palace
Formose: Beautiful
Fougeres: Brackens or ferns
Garnitures de Toilette Epines: Thorn beds
Glycines: Wisteria
Goujon: A type of fish
Grande Boule Lierre: Large ball of ivy
Grande Nue Socle Lierre: Large ivy pedestal
Grenade: Pomegranate fruit
Grimpereaux: Climbers
Grives: Thrushes
Gros Bourdon: Large bumblebee
Gros Poisson Algues: Large fish, algae or seaweed

Guepes: Wasps
Gui: Mistletoe
Guirlandes: Garlands
Hirondelles: Swallows
Honfleur: A French city in Normandy
Ibis: A bird
Jardinee: Garden
Je Reviens: A brand of perfume (the return)
Jeune Faune: Young deer
Koudour: A biblical reference
Lagamar: Brazilian tourism area
L'Air Du Temps: A brand of perfume
Laiterons: Thistles
Languedoc: Language of southern France
Lapin: Rabbit
Laurier: Laurel or wreath
Laussane: A city in Switzerland
Lezard et Bluets: Lizard and flowers
Libellule: Dragonfly
Lierre: Ivy
Louveciennes: A city in France
Lys: Lillies, as in fleur de lys
Malesherbes: A French city south of Paris
Malines: A city in Belgium
Marguerites: Daisies
Martinets: Swifts (birds)
Martinique: An island in the Caribbean colonized by France
Medici: A famous European family
Meduse: Jellyfish
Mesange: Titmouse
Moineau Coquet, Moineau Hardi, Moineau Moqueur: Three figures of sparrows
Moissac: A French city known for its medieval architecture
Molsheim: A French village known for its culture
Monnaie Du Pape: A large flowering plant, "currency of the pope"
Montargis: A French city near Paris
Moyenne Voilee: Middle sail
Muguet: Lily of the valley
Myrrhis: A perennial herb
Mystere: Mystery
Naiades: Water nymphs
Nefliers: Medlar trees
Nemours: A French city
Oleron: A French island
Ondes: Waves
Ondines: Water sprites
Oeuvres de Lalique: Works of Lalique
Oree: Edge of a wood
Origan: Oregano spice
Ormeaux: Elm trees
Ornis: Ash trees
Oursin: Sea urchin
Palerme: Palermo, Italy
Palissy: Picket fence
Pan: Piece or section, also a mythical character

Panneaux: Panels
Papillons: Butterflies
Paquerette: Daisy
Panier de Fruits: Basket of fruit
Panier de Roses: Basket of roses
Pavots D'Argent: Puppies of silver
Pendentif Feuilles a Baies: Pendant of leaves and berries
Pendentif Figurine a Glycine: Pendant of a figure with wisteria
Penthievre: The coast of Brittany
Perche: Perch
Perdrix Couchee: Crouching partridge
Perdrix Debout: Upright partridge
Perigord: A French region of caves and castles
Perles: Pearls
Perruches: Chatterboxes
Picardie: A French region along the English Channel
Pinsons: Finches
Pintade: Guinea fowl
Piriac: A coastal city in Brittany
Plumes: Feathers
Poissons: Fish
Primeveres: Primroses

Raisins: Same as English
Rampillon: Site of a 13th century church
Raquette: Racket for tennis
Renommee D'Orsay: A brand of perfume (renommee means famous)
Ronces: Bramble bushes
Rosace: Rose window
Sainte-Christophe: St. Christopher
Saint Nectaire: A French village, also a type of cheese
Salmonides: Salmon fish
Sanglier: Wild boar
Sauge: Meadow sage
Sauterelles: Grasshoppers
Scarabees: Beetles
Semis du Fleurs: Seedbed of flowers
Sirenes: Mermaids
Statuette Drapee: Draped statuette
Soudan: Sudan, an African nation
Souris: Mouse
Source De La Fontaine Calypso: Statuette designed for a monumental fountain that welcomed visitors to the Paris Exposition of 1925
Source De La Fountaine Clytie: Another statuette designed for a monumental

fountain that welcomed visitors to the Paris Exposition of 1925
Taureau: Bull
Telline: A type of shellfish
Tete D'Aigle: Head of an eagle
Tete De Coq: Head of a chicken
Tete D'Epervier: Head of a sparrow hawk
Tete de Paon: Head of a peacock
Tobago: A Caribbean nation
Tortues: Winding or meandering
Tourbillons: Whirlpools
Tournon: Tournament
Tourterelles: Turtle doves
Trefles: Clovers
Tzigane: A Hungarian Gypsy, also a type of music
Unie: United
Vallauris: A city in southern France, also a type of pottery
Veilleuse: Perfume bottle
Vers Toi: Toward you
Vezelay: A city in France
Victoire: Victory
Volubulis: A Moroccan city famous for Roman ruins
Volutes: Scrolls

Resources

This book would not have been possible without the resources and generous assistance of the following:

Laurie and Joel Shapiro

David Rago Auctions, Inc.
333 North Main Street
Lambertville, NJ 08530
(609) 397-9374
http://www.ragoarts.com/contact.html
info@ragoarts.com

Finesse Fine Art
Tony Wraight
Empool Cottage, West Knighton,
Dorchester, Dorset, DT28PE
http://www.fine-art.demon.co.uk/main.htm
tony@finesse-fine-art.com
Tel. +44 (0) 1305-854286
Fax. +44 (0) 1305-852888
Mobile. +44 (0) 7973-886937

NICHOLAS M. DAWES
Antiques Dealer and Lecturer
67 East 11th Street
New York, NY 10003
(212) 473-5111 (phone)
(212) 353-3845 (fax)
nmdawes@aol.com

Antique & Collectors Reproduction News
Mark Chervenka, editor
Box 12130-WS
Des Moines, Iowa 50312
(515) 274-5886
http://www.repronews.com/
acrn@repronews.com

Paul Stamati Gallery
1050 2nd Avenue
New York, N.Y. 10022
Phone: (212) 754-4533
Fax: (212) 754-4552
Web site: stamati.com
E-mail: gallerymail@stamati.com

Kenneth Luebke of Austin, Texas

To see the Lalique collection owned by Prof. Jack Richards of New Zealand,
  visit: http://www.professorjackrichards.com.